John Fraser Macqueen

Chief Points in the Laws of War and Neutrality, Search and Blockade

With the Changes of 1856, and those Now Proposed

John Fraser Macqueen

Chief Points in the Laws of War and Neutrality, Search and Blockade
With the Changes of 1856, and those Now Proposed

ISBN/EAN: 9783337120764

Printed in Europe, USA, Canada, Australia, Japan

Cover: Foto ©ninafisch / pixelio.de

More available books at **www.hansebooks.com**

CHIEF POINTS IN THE LAWS

OF

WAR AND NEUTRALITY,

SEARCH AND BLOCKADE;

WITH

THE CHANGES OF 1856, AND THOSE NOW PROPOSED.

BY

JOHN FRASER MACQUEEN, Esq.,

ONE OF HER MAJESTY'S COUNSEL.

Author of "A Practical Treatise on the Appellate Jurisdiction of the House of Lords and Privy Council," "The Rights and Liabilities of Husband and Wife," and "A Practical Treatise on the Law of Marriage, Divorce, and Legitimacy, as administered in the Divorce Court and in the House of Lords."

RICHMOND:
WEST AND JOHNSTON.
1863.

"Maritime Law in time of war has long been the subject of deplorable disputes."—*Declaration of the Great Powers at Paris, April* 16, 1856.

"Her Majesty's Government wish to establish a doctrine for all time."
—EARL RUSSELL *to the American Envoy Extraordinary,* 28*th August,* 1861.

"The Declaration of Paris in 1856 forms a new era in International Law."—M. HAUTEFEUILLE.

"It is necessary that controverted questions of neutrality, contraband, blockade, and privateering should be disposed of speedily and for ever."—*Examiner,* 22*d December,* 1861.

TO

SIR ROUNDELL PALMER, M. P.,

HER MAJESTY'S SOLICITOR-GENERAL,

THESE

"CHIEF POINTS" OF A SCIENCE

WHICH HE HAS ADVANCED

ARE INSCRIBED.

TABLE OF CONTENTS.

Section I.
Belligerents in the Enemy's Country.

		PAGE
1.	Principle of terror in ancient wars	1
2.	Leniency and forbearance now enjoined	2
3.	The Duke of Wellington's wise practice	2
4.	Count Diebitsch's example	2
5.	Mr. Burke's benignant doctrine	3
6.	Italian war of 1859	3
7.	Marshal Brune's remonstrance against destroying the Dutch dikes	3
8.	Destruction of vines and fruit trees in Afghanistan	4
9.	Destruction of granaries at Odessa	4
10.	Destruction of forts and stores	4
11.	Charleston stone fleet	5
12.	Louis XIV and the Eddystone Lighthouse	5
13.	Consideration for women and children	5
14.	Prisoners of war	6

Section II.
Belligerents in their own Country.

1.	Defensive destruction of property by Peter the Great	7
2.	By the Emperor Alexander	7
3.	By William the Silent	7
4.	By Jacopo del Verme	8
5.	Vindictive destruction of property	8
6.	Vindictive closing of harbors	8
7	Defence of mercantile towns	9
8.	Defence of fortified towns	9

A*

Section III.
Belligerents at Sea.

		PAGE
1.	Capture of enemy's property a duty	9
2.	When capture impracticable, destruction enjoined	10
3.	Marine severities vindicated by jurists	11
4.	Opinion of Lord Clarendon	11
5.	Seizure of fishing-boats	12
6.	Remarkable case before Lord Stowell	12
7.	Indulgence to fishermen granted, but revoked	12
8.	Humane French ordinance	14

Section IV.
Belligerents and Neutrals.

1.	The war must be " regular "	14
2.	Case of the American war in 1780	15
3.	Division into belligerents and neutrals	16
4.	Neutrals must hold the war " just "	16
5.	Asylum to belligerent vessels	17
6.	Rules as to their departure	18
7.	Great duty of neutrals	18
8.	Favor shown to belligerents	18
9.	Neutrals must not assist	19
10.	Neutrals may trade with belligerents, but restrictedly	19
11.	Justice of the restriction examined	20
12.	That fire-arms, etc., prolong war	20
13.	This position examined	20
14.	Opinion of David Hume*	21
	* Opinion of Captain Gulliver	22

Section V.
Search for Contraband of War, etc.

1.	The Queen's proclamation as to contraband	22
2.	Opinions thereon by Lords Ellenborough, Granville, and Kingsdown	23
3.	Provisions deemed contraband	23

CONTENTS. vii

	PAGE
4. Medicinal plants contraband	24
5. Quasi-contraband: men, dispatches, etc.,	24
6. Lord Stowell's comprehensive principle	24
7. Stoppage and search for contraband	25
8. Consequences of search for contraband	25
9. When there is doubt as to contraband	25
10. Sale and conveyance of contraband not an offence in the neutral state	25
11. Visit to ascertain nationality	26

Section VI.
Blockades.

1. Blockades	27
2. Their principle examined*	27
3. They should be real	29
4. The real blockade has limits	30
5. Ought blockades to be abolished?	30
6. Severe penalties for the breach of them	30
7. Essentials of blockade in the present day	32
8. Test of sufficiency	32
9. Intermissions and revivals of blockade	33
10. Blockades without captures	33
11. Would blockades without captures be effective?	34

* Note as to the Roman Civil Law.

Section VII.
The Prize Jurisdiction.

1. Opinion of Lord Stowell in 1799	35
2. His opinion in 1812	35
3. These opinions contrasted	37
4. The Court has two masters	37
5. Serious consequence	37
6. Lord Stowell's position difficult	38
7. Lord Stowell severe on neutrals	41
8. Lord Stowell indulgent to captors	41

		PAGE
9.	Prize money awarded to captors	42
10.	Temptation to random captures	43
11.	Correction of Lord Stowell's law	43

Section VIII.
Late Changes in the Maritime Law of Nations.

1.	The Paris Solemn Declarations	44
2.	How far they bind	45
3.	Privateering abolished	46
4.	Effect on America	46
5.	Enemy's goods safe under neutral flag	47
6.	Lord Derby's apprehensions	49
7.	Lord Palmerston's good auguries	49
8.	Case put by Lord Derby	50
9.	Answer by Lord Granville	50
10.	Neutral goods safe under enemy's flag	51
11.	What blockades bind by the Paris declaration	51
12.	Variance by the Queen's proclamation	51

Section IX.
Proposed Changes in the Maritime Law of Nations.

1.	Ought private property to be respected at sea?*	52
2.	America always for immunity	54
3.	Opinion of Napoleon I	55
4.	Lord Palmerston	56
5.	What the policy of Great Britain	57
6.	Opinion of the mercantile body	58
7.	Report of Commons' Committee	58
8.	Opinion of Earl Russell	59
9.	Conclusion	60
	* Protocol as to mediation to prevent war	53

Section X.

POSTSCRIPT.

Showing the present state of sentiment in the House of Commons, as to securing an immunity for all private property at sea, during hostilities.

		PAGE
1.	Opinion of Mr. Horsfall	61
2.	the Attorney-General	62
3.	Mr. Liddell	63
4.	Mr. B. Cochrane	63
5.	Sir G. Bowyer	63
6.	G. C. Lewis	64
7.	Mr. Baring	65
8.	Mr. Lindsay	66
9.	the Lord Advocate	67
10.	Sir S. Northcote	67
11.	Mr. Gower	69
12.	Mr. Cave	69
13.	Sir F. Goldsmidt	69
14.	Lord H. Vane	70
15.	Mr. Buxton	70
16.	Mr. Newdegate	70
17.	Mr. Massey	71
18.	Mr. Bentinck	72
19.	Mr. Bright	72
20.	the Solicitor-General	74
21.	Mr. Walpole	79
22.	Lord Palmerston	80
23.	Mr. Disraeli	81

APPENDIX.

	PAGE
The Paris Solemn Declaration of April, 16, 1856	82
The Queen's Proclamation, 13th May, 1861	84
Sir Roundell Palmer's Speech on the Effect of the Queen's Proclamation	87
The Queen's Waiver of Right on the Eve of the Russian War, 28th March, 1854	92
Sir William Molesworth's Speech on the Neutral Flag	93
INDEX	97

CHIEF POINTS IN THE LAWS

OF

WAR AND NEUTRALITY,

ETC.

The Law of Nations during war has many admirable propositions, which we trust will never be disturbed. It has also some questionable maxims. These last must be examined with reverence, but with freedom.

My purpose is to state shortly the chief points, to put forward here and there a suggestion, and to leave to the reader's judgment the decision.

I begin with the rules which ought to govern belligerents in their enemy's country. The other divisions will be taken in the order of the preceding table.

Section I.

Belligerents in the Enemy's Country.

1. In ancient times an invading army, to inspire terror, sought the earliest opportunity of displaying its severity. The slaughter of those who held out was vindicated on the ground that destroying one garri- *[Principle of terror in ancient wars.]*

son without mercy might prevent others from resisting, and so save the effusion of blood. To this sophistry, Lord Brougham tells us, the answer is obvious: for that by the same reasoning war might be proved innocent in proportion to its cruelty.*

2. Vattel, the great authority of the last century, enjoins leniency and forbearance. <small>Leniency and forbearance now enjoined.</small> He denounces the laying waste of the Palatinate by Turenne. And the truth is that cruelty, pillage, and marauding, though practised largely in the first Napoleon's wars, have no sanction from any modern jurist.

3. Our illustrious Duke of Wellington punished all predatory aggressions committed by his troops.† <small>The Duke of Wellington's wise practice.</small> He made them pay their way. The protection of the inhabitants from wanton injury he considered a high duty, and, for evident reasons, the best policy. The French more than once felt, to their cost, the effects of an opposite line of conduct.

4. When Count Diebitsch with his Russian army entered Roumelia, in 1829, he gave a shining example of military clemency. <small>Count Diebitsch's example.</small> He assured the Mussulmans that they should be safe in their persons and property; and that he would not disturb either the exercise of their religion, or the course of their civil admin-

---

* England and France under House of Lancaster, p. 206.

† The proof of this is everywhere: but chiefly in his advances into France, in spring 1814, and to Paris, in July, 1815. See Sir Archibald Alison's great work.

istration; but he required them to deliver up their arms, as a deposit, to be restored on the return of peace.

5. The conduct of this humane Russian commander harmonizes with a benignant doctrine stated by an illustrious writer: "Upon the taking of a town, or the subjection of a province, it is usual among civilized nations to afford protection and full security to the inhabitants; and such of them as do not choose to live under the new government are allowed a reasonable time to dispose of their lands and effects, and to depart in all safety."* _{Mr. Burke's benignant doctrine.}

6. In the Italian war of 1859, remarkable for the enormous bodies of troops assembled, "we are told that the two hostile armies passed over the richest plains in Europe, leaving behind them little trace of their presence, except on the actual battle-fields."† _{Italian war of 1859.}

7. Marshal Brune, a jurist, and a man of literature before he became a soldier, stated to the Duke of York, in 1799, during an armistice in Holland, "that if the duke should cause the dikes to be destroyed, and the country to be inundated, when not useful to his own army or detrimental to the enemy's, it would be contrary to the laws of war, and must draw upon him the reprobation of all Europe."‡ _{Marshal Brune's remonstrance against destroying the Dutch dikes.}

---

* Dodsley's Annual Register, 1772, p. 37, drawn up by Mr. Burke.
† See an able pamphlet on "Maritime Capture, by a Lawyer." Ridgway, 1862.
‡ 1 Kent's Comm. 92.

The proposed exploit, if the story be true, was in imitation of Louis XIV's accomplished one, which procured for that king, as Voltaire says, the "deplorable glory of having destroyed one of the master-pieces of human industry."

8. The destruction of the vines and fruit-trees in Afghanistan, a serious injury to that country without any corresponding benefit to the invaders, was undoubtedly a breach of the laws of war.

Destruction of vines and fruit-trees in Afghanistan.

9. In bombarding Odessa, the English and French powers did their best to save the granaries, not merely from considerations of humanity, but also from a regard to the law of nations: every country in Europe deriving benefit from those stores. This ground was expressly taken by the Emperor Nicholas, when he complained that factories, warehouses, and shops had been destroyed.

Destruction of granaries at Odessa.

10. We can understand why private property, instruments of husbandry, and every article of a peaceful character, and more especially, why churches, temples, libraries, pictures, statues, and public monuments are invariably spared in war. But how as to fortified places and military stores? The case of Almeida raises this question. There General Brienne, having determined to cut his way through the British besieging forces, determined also, as a preliminary, to destroy the fortress, with all its military stores. This double operation he executed with an ability and success commended by Colonel

Destruction of forts and stores.

Napier.* But General Sarrazin, in his history of the Spanish campaign, expresses an opinion that the destruction of the fort and stores of Almeida was a violation of the laws of war. We should have thought that it was a laudable achievement, otherwise it would seem that the common practice of spiking artillery is indefensible.

11. But what shall we say as to the late operation at Charleston? The Stone Fleet, if intended to be a permanent impediment to commerce, may justly be regarded as a world-wide injury, and consequently a breach of the law of nations. *(Charleston stone fleet.)*

12. During Queen Anne's wars a French privateer seized the workmen employed in erecting Rudyerd's Lighthouse on the Eddystone Rock, and carried them off as prisoners; but Louis XIV immediately ordered their release, bestowed on them presents, and sent them back to their duty, declaring that "although he was at war with England he was not at war with mankind." *(Louis XIV and the Eddystone Lighthouse.)*

13. Dr. Phillimore† tells us that at Sebastopol "the English general refused to abstain from firing upon a particular quarter said to be inhabited by women and children, but he offered them a free passage beyond the lines of the army." *(Consideration for women and children.)*

---

* See Napier's Peninsular War. † Int. Law, vol. iii, p. 112.

14. The old rule was that prisoners of war became the slaves of the victor, who had the power of life and death. At Rome the more distinguished were reserved for the triumph, and butchered afterward. Contrary cases are mentioned as wonders. In the days of chivalry the hope of ransom alone caused quarter to be given.* The vanquished Sultan Bajazet was carried about in a cage.† Bynkershoek, the great jurist, writing not far from our own time, defends the hanging of prisoners. But in modern warfare between Christian nations mercy is shown, and everything done to soften the mishap of a brave enemy. This appears on both sides in the Crimean contest. At the battle of Solferino, the Emperor of the French gave orders that the wounded Austrians should be treated precisely as if they were his own soldiers.

Prisoners of war.

---

* See *Henry V*, Act. iv, scene 4, where Pistol exacts "egregious ransom," under the last penalty.

† The disputed cruelty of Timour — a savage and an infidel — was surpassed by the authentic and more recent cruelty of a renowned Christian prince, Bedford, the brother of Henry V, under whose auspices Joan of Arc — a prisoner of war in the truest sense of the phrase — was exhibited to the populace in an iron cage on her way to Rouen, where she was burnt alive. The story is too shocking to read. The excuse is that Joan was considered a sorceress. Lord Brougham, in the excellent book already cited, shows that the French were more to blame in this affair than the English; pp. 221 to 297.

Section II.

Belligerents in their own Country.

1. Let us next inquire, how far during war is a government entitled to destroy, or mutilate its own territory, and the property of individuals thereon? Vattel thinks that even here there is a limit.* He is of opinion that the policy of Peter the Great, who laid waste eighty leagues of his empire in order to arrest the progress of Charles XII, could be justified by nothing short of an imperious necessity. Defensive destruction of property by Peter the Great.

2. So, on the French jurist's authority, we may lay it down that the course taken by Alexander required the like excuse, when he made a desert, and fired Moscow for the reception of Napoleon. Such violent remedies, even though defensive, are not often to be resorted to. Vattel holds that a prince who without the strongest grounds should imitate the example of Peter the Great, would be justly culpable in the eyes of his own countrymen. Whether other nations might complain he does not say. By the Emperor Alexander.

3. In 1573 William the Silent cut the dikes round Leyden, then besieged by the Spaniards. The land was laid under water, and the crops were swallowed up. It was an extreme step, but justified by necessity and by success. The tide destroyed the besieging army, and brought up the Zealand fleet laden with pro- By William the Silent.

---

* Lib. 3, c. 9, § 167.

visions for the famishing inhabitants. Thus Leyden was saved.

4. Nearly two centuries before, when the duties of belligerents in their own country were less understood, or less attended to than in the days of William the Silent, Jacopo del Verme, apparently without necessity, and certainly without success, cut the dikes of the Adige, in the hope of destroying the Florentine army, commanded by Sir John Hawkwood; but that skilful leader effected a retreat, without material loss, leaving the Milanese to deplore their useless sacrifice of territory.*

<small>By Jacopo del Verme.</small>

5. An injury to ourselves may be an injury to others. If, when the English and French bombarded Odessa, the Russians had vindictively destroyed its corn-magazines, a question might have arisen whether such an act was not contrary to the laws of war.

<small>Vindictive destruction of property.</small>

6. Suppose a dangerous sea-coast, extended hundreds of miles, with only one harbor. Are we to entertain a doubt that the world at large has a right to exact the benefit of that harbor? The owners of the soil have but a qualified property in it. This extreme case tries the principle, and shows its irresistible authority. We cannot always do what we will with our own.

<small>Vindictive closing of harbors.</small>

7. To defend an unfortified mercantile town,

---

* Poggio Bracciolini, Hist. Florent.; Sismondi, Hist. Rep. Ital.

completely invested by the enemy, has been held a breach of the laws of war, because such a case is one for honorable surrender—to prevent useless carnage and the unavailing destruction of property. *(Defence of mercantile towns.)*

8. On the 30th August, 1759, the Austrian forces, having finally established their batteries around Breslau, sent a message to Count Tavenzien, who commanded the town, reminding him that as it was a mercantile place, not a fortress, he could not defend it without contravening the laws of war. The count, in the character of a military jurisconsult, admitted the law, but denied the fact; affirming that "Breslau, being surrounded by military works and wet ditches, was a place of strength, and not merely a mercantile town.* He therefore called upon the Austrians to do their worst. *(Defence of fortified towns.)*

Section III.

Belligerents at Sea.

1. We should have expected that the humane and just principles applied to property on land would also be applied to property at sea. But this is not so. On the contrary, all property, public or private, belonging to the enemy, if found in an enemy's *(Capture of enemy's property a duty.)*

---

* Dodsley's Annual Register, 1760, p. 18, drawn up by Mr. Burke.

ship at sea, or in port afloat, is liable to capture. In other words, what is prohibited on land is perfectly allowable, and is in fact prescribed as a duty, at sea.*

2. But even at sea we are not to appropriate or to destroy the enemy's property, *brevi manu:* there must be an adjudication. Hence, it is a violation of the maritime code to burn merchant ships instead of taking them to a prize court. At the same time it is to be remembered that the captors may not always be able to take the ship into port. In such a case, Lord Stowell said that the "captors could not, consistently with their general duty to their own country, or indeed its express injunctions, permit enemy's property to sail away unmolested — if impossible to bring in, their next duty is to destroy it."† There are other authorities to the same effect. Indeed, Dr. Lushington, in "The Leucade,"‡ lays it down that "the destruction of a vessel under hostile colors is a matter of duty;" and that "the bringing of an enemy's vessel to adjudication is not called for by any respect to the right of the enemy proprietor."

When capture impracticable, destruction enjoined.

3. Still, the question remains — on what princi-

---

* The inoffensive mercantile mariners navigating the vessel, and all others on board (being of the hostile nation), are on capture of the ship made prisoners of war, and, if necessary, put under hatches. Sometimes they are handcuffed; but it is not usual (according to the mildness of modern practice) to put them in irons, though on a late occasion this was done.

† 2 Dodson, 381.

‡ 2 Spinks Ecc. & Adm. 231.

ple of justice is the property of peaceful merchants liable to capture at sea, while the very same property, belonging to the very same individuals, if found on land, would be treated with forbearance? The jurists do not explain why this should be. Chancellor Kent* tells us "that there is a marked difference in the rights of war carried on by land and by sea;" adding that "the object of a maritime war is the destruction of the enemy's commerce and navigation, in order to weaken and destroy the foundation of his naval power;" but that "the usage is not to touch property on land without making compensation." He assigns no reason for the distinction. It is scarcely a satisfactory solution to say that the general use of maritime insurance casts losses at sea on those who by contract are bound to sustain them. *Marine severities vindicated by jurists.*

4. An eminent statesman,† after observing that "by land we should think it disgraceful to seize the property of peaceful persons, even subjects of the enemy," adverts to the difference of the rule at sea, and declares that there is no assignable reason for the distinction, "except, perhaps, that acts committed at sea are less under observation than those committed on land; and the force of opinion is, consequently, less brought to bear on the former." *Opinion of Lord Clarendon.*

---

* Vol. i. p. 107. See also Wheaton's Elements, p. 429, and *Hansard*, 14 July, 1857, where Lord John Russell says, "the comparison between private property in ships and private property on land is not tenable."

† Lord Clarendon.—*Hansard*, 22d May, 1856.

5. Not only is it the practice to capture and condemn as lawful prize the enemy's merchantmen and cargoes, but during our later wars with France and Holland we condescended to humbler booty: for we seized the boats of French and Dutch fishermen, who plied their precarious industry upon our coasts, and we treated them exactly as if they were prosecuting, not a harmless and useful, but a criminal occupation.

<small>Seizure of fishing-boats.</small>

6. Lord Stowell seems to have pronounced judgment with but little satisfaction in a case of this description which came before the prize court on the 13th November, 1798. A small fishing-vessel having been captured by British cruisers on her return from the Dogger Bank to Holland with a cargo of cod, his lordship delivered the following opinion—

<small>Remarkable case before Lord Stowell.</small>

"In former wars it has not been usual to make captures of these small fishing-vessels; but this was a rule of comity only, and not of legal decision; it has prevailed from views of mutual accommodation between neighboring countries, and from tenderness to a poor and industrious order of people. In the present war there has, I presume, been sufficient reason for changing this mode of treatment; and as they are brought before me for my judgment, they must be referred to the general principles of this court; they fall under the character and description of ships constantly and exclusively employed in the enemy's trade."—*Condemnation.*

7. It would appear that shortly after the above decision (and possibly through the intervention of Lord Stowell) some indulgence was vouchsafed to the French fish-

<small>Indulgence to fishermen granted, but revoked.</small>

ermen; but it also appears that from this indulgence evil consequences arose, or were supposed to have arisen. Belsham gives the following account*—

"On the 21st of January, 1801, Mr. Secretary Dundas apprised the Lords of the Admiralty that it was his majesty's pleasure to revoke the indulgence granted to the French fishermen; and that they and their boats should be henceforth subject to capture—advices having been received that these fishermen were under requisition, and that even those who had been released from prison, in order to be sent home, on the express condition of not serving again, were comprised in that requisition. It was his majesty's further pleasure that all those set at liberty on their parole be required to return into this country; and that those among them who shall neglect to obey these orders shall be made to suffer all the rigors of the laws of war, in case they should again be made prisoners while serving the enemies of his majesty. M. Otto, on the 29th of January, immediately apprised M. Talleyrand of this measure, the true motives of which he declared himself unable to conjecture; at the same time expressing his fears that, from the intentional delay in the communication of the order, a great number of unfortunate persons must have fallen victims to it. M. Otto also addressed a reply to the British government, deprecating 'a measure hostile to a peaceable class of people, for the most part, aged, invalids, or children, who were consequently incapable of hurting the enemies of their country; and whose simplicity of manners and industrious habits could not give any umbrage.' This act of provocation awakened the highest resentment in the First Consul, who sent instructions to M. Otto to declare to the British government, that the French government, could not, on its part, think of making the poor fishermen victims of the prolongation of hostility, and therefore, that it would abstain from reprisals, having

margin: Fishermen released on parole.

margin: Indignation of the First Consul.

---

* Hist. of Eng., vol. xii, p. 169.

given orders that all French ships, armed for war or cruising, should leave the occupation of fishermen undisturbed."

8. It is remarkable that a French ordinance issued so far back as 1543 gave protection to fishermen during hostilities. It was obeyed till the time of Louis XIV, but afterward fell into disuse, owing to the ill-faith exhibited, as Valin affirms, "by the enemies of France." The ancient and excellent ordinance thus neglected may now perhaps be regarded as the germ of a better policy; though, when we look at the date of it, we may be apt to think that the world does not always advance in humanity as it advances in civilization.

<small>Humane French ordinance.</small>

Section IV.

Belligerents and Neutrals.

1. The war must be what is called in the language of international law a *regular* war. It may be between two separate states, by the sovereign authority of each; or it may be between one portion of a state and another portion of the same state. Suppose a rebellion, or a clamor for secession. Let us take rebellion first. It involves a civil war. Of this nature was the revolt of the low countries against Spain, three centuries ago. No one disputed that the most cruel of all contests which then ensued between sovereign and subject was orthodox, so far as neutrals were concerned, how-

<small>The war must be "regular."</small>

ever much it violated the municipal code. It was not for the world at large to await the recognition of the tyrannical Philip.* Then as to secession. The attempt may be illegal. The actors may be traitors. But at a necessary period the law of nations will step in to define and to fix the rights and duties of the belligerents relatively to neutrals. At all events, we must hold that ever since the date of Queen Victoria's proclamation† the unhappy civil war now raging in America has been *regular*. The Federal government itself, both by conduct and by direct appeal, has invoked the law of nations, which, where it properly applies, must be accepted by all; but it does not follow that the municipal relations are displaced as between the belligerents. The Southern insurgents may be rebels, and may continue rebels, till their rebellion has succeeded or has been suppressed.

2. After describing Lord Cornwallis' severities in South Carolina, Mr. Massey says:‡ "The American insurgents, once they had been admitted to the privileges of civilized warfare, could no longer be dealt with as rebels." This proposition, though just and generous, seems doubtful in point of law. It was not until subsequently to the South Carolina severities that the American conflict received, from the King's speech, opening Parliament in No-

Case of the American war in 1780.

---

* Lord Brougham's Political Philosophy, vol. iii, 375.
† 13th May, 1861.   ‡ Hist. of Geo. III, vol. iii, 26.

vember, 1780, the title of "a war." Prior to that speech, it was a rebellion; and it was so studiously described and treated by the British government. The present American insurgents were pronounced rebels by the Secretary-at-War in the House of Commons, on the 11th of March, 1862. What the law is, is one thing. It is a very different consideration whether its penalties should be enforced. Upon the question of policy and humanity, all must agree with Mr. Massey. But let us not forget that although the rebellion of 1745 had every mark of civilization, especially on the part of the vanquished, the chief of them were executed on Tower Hill for their treason.

3. Supposing the war to be regular, the law of nations divides mankind into two classes, belligerents and neutrals. A and B are belligerents, at war with each other. All the other letters of the alphabet are bystanders, that is to say, neutrals, looking on, but taking no part in the fray.

Division into belligerents and neutrals.

4. It is a maxim that so long as the established rules are observed, the war, being regular, must in the eyes of neutrals be deemed a *just* war, which the jurists rather oddly explain to mean just on both sides.*

Neutrals must hold the war "just."

---

* "Les guerres doivent être réputées justes de la part des deux belligérants."—HAUTEFEUILLE, *Des Droits et des Devoirs des Nations Neutres*, lit. 3, chap. 1, s. 2, vol. 1, 133, 2de édit. Vattel says, "*La guerre en forme, quant à ses effets, doit être regardée comme juste de part et d'autre.*"—B. 3, c. 12, § 190. Vattel says "this is absolutely necessary." But it would rather appear to be a superfluous refinement. In another place Vattel affirms with great truth that "a war *cannot* be just on both sides."—B. 3, c. 3, § 39.

They are not satisfied with saying that neutrals have nothing to do with the merits of the belligerents' quarrel. The jurists insist that neutrals shall blindly "accept the facts without discussing them." We know, however, from recent observation, that neutrals disregard this injunction. They never do accept the facts without discussing them. On the contrary, they examine the facts critically, discuss them copiously, and form their opinions upon them freely. But it does not follow that because they may deem the war unjust, or absurd, they are on that account to interfere and put an end to it. They have no high duty to perform. They may look on with composure. It is enough that they submit patiently to the humiliations and disadvantages which, as will appear by and by, are abundantly cast upon them by the maritime law of nations.

5. Neutral nations usually give an asylum in their ports to the ships of both belligerents; and we have seen this done recently under circumstances which might, perhaps, have justified a refusal of the favor. *Asylum belligerent vessels.*

To grant such an asylum to one belligerent, and refuse it to another, would be, to use the language of the jurists, unneutral. The belligerents have no right to ask the benefit of neutral ports, or roadsteads; but in the case of storms, or pressure of any kind, to deny refuge would be uncharitable and unchristian; and there is authority for holding that it would be contrary to the law of nations.

6. When two vessels, hostile to each other, meet in a neutral port, or when one pursues the other into a neutral port, they must behave themselves peaceably while there. Should one of them sail away, the other must not follow until after twenty-four hours have elapsed. One object of this regulation is to prevent any reasonable chance of collision upon the coast.

Rules as to their departure.

7. In time of war, the great study of surrounding nations is to abstain diligently from doing anything that may interrupt the proceeding of the combatants. However great the inconvenience, the rule is that states not engaged in the conflict shall permit it to proceed without impediment, without remonstrance, and without complaint. Courtesy so elevated and so refined does not exist in private life; for, when we see two men fighting in the street, our first impulse is to separate them, especially if the match be unequal. Should they resist our importunities, and by persevering stop the thoroughfare, we call in the police, who at once take charge of the offenders.

Great duty of neutrals.

8. To these simple dictates of reason and justice the law of nations, as now established, does not accede.* That law accords to belligerents certain rights, or rather high privileges, uniformly vexatious and

Favor shown to belligerents.

---

* It may, perhaps, be doubted whether, in the case of small, insignificant states, the rule of private life would not be applied. Great states have license—or take it.

often deeply mischievous to neutrals, whose only remedy is submission. Belligerents are, in fact, favorites of the maritime law, which seems to frown on all who are at peace with their fellow men. Why, or how, this should be, is not easy to explain satisfactorily. The doctrine arose in remote and barbarous ages; but our chief difficulty is to understand how, with all its oppressive incidents, it has been so long acquiesced in. "Let us inquire," says a distinguished modern jurist, "what is the nature of this exorbitant right of belligerents? For what purpose has it been created? and what are its proper limitations?"

9. The law requires that neutrals shall not assist either of the belligerents. If they do, they cease to be neutrals, and become principals. This is reasonable.

Neutrals must not assist.

10. Neutrals, however, are not interdicted from trading with belligerents. They may maintain their commercial relations with A and B; in other words, with either, or with both of the belligerents. This being so, suppose a merchant, in the ordinary course of his business, transmits arms and ammunition to A. This will be a hazardous adventure; for arms and ammunition so sent to A may injure B, and therefore it is open to B, as the law stands, to capture and confiscate both the ship and the cargo. So, in like manner, let us suppose that the same merchant, in the same course of business, sends arms and ammunition to the opposite belligerent, B. Here it will be competent

Neutrals may trade with belligerents, but restrictedly.

to A (as it was in the other case to B) to capture and confiscate both the ship and the cargo.

11. But is it not a fair question for considera-
<small>Justice of the restriction examined.</small> tion, whether an act performed in the ordinary, legitimate course of commerce can reasonably be deemed a breach of neutrality? The merchant pursues his lawful avocation. Regardless of the war, he looks only to his profits. The belligerents, in his eyes, are customers, and he hopes they are solvent. He deals indifferently with A, or with B, or with both, in the systematic prosecution of his honorable calling. If one belligerent derives more benefit from commerce than another, it is because his resources are greater, and not because neutrality has been violated. His superiority in this respect is a source of strength, and an element of success, which the other belligerent ought to have considered before entering on the contest.

12. The jurists, however, take another ground.
<small>That fire-arms, etc., prolong war.</small> They affirm that supplies of arms and ammunition prolong the war; a mischief which is not obviated, but increased, by accommodating both parties alike.

13. Now, is it quite certain that supplies of
<small>This position examined.</small> arms and ammunition have really the effect of lengthening the contest? Are they not more likely to abridge it? What is the best recommendation of our modern improvements in gunnery, and of the general advance which has recently been made in the military art? Beyond all question, *this*—that they accelerate the

result, and, on the whole, diminish the sacrifice of human life. Sir William Armstrong is a public benefactor, and has been rewarded as such. The Minie rifle, which kills at a thousand yards, is a meritorious invention. If we had had only bows and arrows and battering rams in the Crimea, when would Sebastopol have been taken? One of our wars with France lasted a hundred years. This could hardly have happened had the true capabilities of fire-arms, especially of artillery, been then understood.*

14. The most sagacious of historians, Mr. Hume,† remarks that artillery, "though it seems contrived for the destruction of mankind, has in the issue rendered war much less bloody, for by its means nations have been brought more to a level," and peaceful consummations are more rapidly accomplished. This great writer commends as a social improvement the happy invention of gunpowder, war's first instrument, but the most powerful of all

<small>Opinion David Hume.</small>

---

* The above suggestions are well supported by the *Standard* of 4th February, 1862, in the following pointed sentences: "Napoleon overran Italy in a month, and conquered Prussia in a week. The Duke of Wellington marched out of Portugal on May 22, 1813; fought the battle of Vittoria on June 21; and before the end of the month there was not a Frenchman left in Spain. So there were but three months from Elba to Waterloo. Napoleon III met the Austrians first at Magenta, on June 3, 1859, and finished the campaign at Solferino in less than a month." What, then, becomes of the jurists' assertion that "arms and ammunition prolong the war?"

† Hist. vol. ii, 466.

agents in hastening its termination.* The reasoning of the jurists, therefore, on this fundamental point, proceeds on a debatable basis, and calls for further examination. That reasoning, whether right or wrong (I offer no opinion either way), is unquestionably the parent of the celebrated doctrine called "contraband of war;" a doctrine which will be considered in the next section, and to which, by recent and coming events, great interest has been imparted.

Section V.

Search for Contraband of War, etc.

1. The Queen's proclamation† as to contraband of war has for its object, not to guarantee evenhandedness to the belligerents, but to keep out of trouble her own people. It warns her majesty's loving subjects that they abstain from

The Queen's proclamation as to contraband.

"Carrying officers, soldiers, dispatches, arms, military stores,

---

* The efficacy of gunpowder, as a pacificator, is more powerfully described by Captain Gulliver than by any other writer. In his advice to the King of Brobdignag, he says: "I told his majesty that I know the ingredients very well, and the manner of compounding them; and that I could direct his workmen how to make hollow tubes of brass or iron, of a size proportionable to all other things in his majesty's kingdom, and the largest need not be above a hundred feet long; twenty or thirty of which tubes, charged with the proper quantity of powder and balls, would batter down the walls of the strongest town *in a few hours.*" The king, whom the captain describes as narrow-minded, rejected this proposal.

Opinion of Captain Gulliver.

† *Infra*, 91.

or materials, or any article or articles considered and deemed to be contraband of war according to the law or modern usage of nations, for the use or service of either of the said contending parties."

2. On the 16th of May, 1861, the following remarks fell from the peers in Parliament—

<small>Opinions thereon by Lords Ellenborough, Granville, and Kingsdown.</small>

Lord Ellenborough: "I regret to see so much vagueness in the expressions used as to contraband of war. How are plain men to find out what articles have of late been so considered by the usage of nations? What are the further articles not mentioned? The law with respect to contraband of war is in a state of constant change. I recollect to have found in the law-books of best authority, that all these changes were controlled by one prevailing principle, namely, that *that* is contraband which, in the possession of an enemy, would enable him better to carry on the war."

Earl Granville: "The government has followed the usual course. Contraband of war must vary according to the character of the war. The decisions of a prize court, unless there has been a flagrant violation of international law, all those who have recognized the rights of the belligerents must accept."

Lord Kingsdown: "The determination of what is contraband must depend on the circumstances of each particular case. Provisions, if sent to a port where an army is in want of food, might become contraband."

3. We know that England detained neutral vessels going to France with corn, meal, and flour, because these articles were eminently calculated to avert starvation. <small>Provisions deemed contraband.</small>
"The situation of France was such as to lead to that mode of distressing her;" so said Mr. Hammond on behalf of the British government, in 1703.

4. It is difficult to believe, what however is

asserted, that in the exercise of our belligerent rights we "endeavored to deprive the enemy's hospitals of one of the most healing plants which Providence has bestowed on suffering mortals."*

<small>Medicinal plants contraband.</small>

5. Besides contraband *proper*, there are cases of *quasi*-contraband, applicable to persons and dispatches. Both are subject to the same discretionary principle, leaving it very much, if not entirely, for the judge to decide what does and what does not involve the legal penalty.†

<small>Quasi-contraband men, dispatches, etc.</small>

6. "It will be sufficient," says Lord Stowell, "if there is an injury arising to the belligerent from the employment in which the vessel is found. The master may be ignorant and perfectly innocent. But if the service is injurious, *that* will be sufficient to give the belligerent a right to prevent the thing from being done."‡ This a foreign jurist calls the *ad libitum* doctrine. The declaration of 1856, to

<small>Lord Stowell's comprehensive principle.</small>

---

* *Edinb. Rev.* of 1812.

† See Dr. Pratt's valuable treatise on Contraband of War; and Mr. C. Clark's disquisition on the Trent case.

‡ 6 Rob. 430. It is not clear that the above are detached dicta. But if they are, they are Lord Stowell's. He revised his judgments, first in manuscript and afterward repeatedly in print. The reports in fact are not the reporter's, but the judge's. Even when at the bar, Lord Stowell began with written speeches. Everything he delivered had a literary finish. In the decisions of this judge, no hasty dicta are to be found. See Rush, Sec. Ser., vol. i, 15. The decisions of Lord Stowell are not in every hand; but the best of them are given by Mr. Tudor in his Leading Cases on Mercantile and Maritime Law. See, also, the Manual of Maritime Warfare, by Messrs. Hazlitt and Roche.

which we will advert hereafter,* does not define contraband of war.

7. That declaration is also silent as to the rights of stoppage† and of search. The belligerent, therefore, must either renounce these rights, or humble every neutral ship by their exercise; for without stoppage, and without search, he cannot ascertain whether the neutral has, or has not contraband on board. Stoppage and search for contraband.

8. When the belligerent finds contraband on board, he will of course take the ship into port; but he must bear in mind Lord Stowell's humane injunction, "not to handcuff the crew, or put them in irons, except in extreme cases."‡ If he find no contraband, he permits the ship to proceed on her voyage. Consequences of search for contraband.

9. Suppose the result of the search to inspire a doubt: in that case the belligerent commander, having a duty to perform, will reserve the doubt for the judge, and take the neutral vessel into port. When there is doubt as to contraband.

10. In every belligerent state the conveyance to the enemy of contraband articles is treated as a delinquincy. But it is not so regarded in the neutral state. Thus, notwithstanding the Queen's proclamation, a British merchant may now lawfully sell contraband articles to an American purchaser; nay, he Sale and conveyance of contraband not an offence in the neutral state.

---

* *Infra*, 45, 89.

† The approved mode of stoppage is by cannon shot—le coup de cannon de semonce.

‡ The San Juan Baptista, 5 Rob. 33; The Die Fire Damer, ib. 357.

may even carry them to New York or to Charleston, if he chooses to run the risk of seizure *in transitu.**

<small>Visit to ascertain nationality.</small>

11. In the last number of the "Edinburgh Review,"† there is an able and candid article on "belligerents and neutrals." It advises the retention of the "right of visitation on the high seas to ascertain the true *national character* of mercantile ships." This is quite distinct from the right of search for contraband; although the mode of proceeding is the same. The reviewer thus describes it—

"The visit is made by an officer in uniform, who proceeds peaceably to the merchant vessel in a boat manned by two or three men besides the rowers, and retires when his lawful inquiries are satisfied."

The writer next observes that what is done is "analogous to the production of a passport by travellers on the Continent;" but—to omit the considerations which have brought passports somewhat into disfavor lately—it must be remembered that the exaction of them assumes sovereignty. There is no sovereign on the high seas.

---

* See all this admirably explained in Sir Roundell Palmer's speech, of the 20th of February, 1862, *infra*, p. 94.

† January, 1862.

Section VI.

Blockades.

1. Superior in rank to the right of stoppage on the high seas is the right of blockading an enemy's port—the most singular of the belligerents' many startling prerogatives. This operation is performed and maintained without the slightest regard to the injury which may thereby be occasioned to neutrals, the great object being to cut off all communication between those who are within and those who are without the place beset. Access and egress are equally deemed offences: not wrongs, but crimes. A blockade is said to be "an act of sovereignty," though why it should be so specially is not explained. It is also called "a conquest." But it may be asked whether it is not rather an act of forcible occupation—a trespass, precarious in tenure, and transient in duration; in truth, without anything to justify it but power. Be this, however, as it may, the Queen's proclamation* charges and commands her loving subjects that they abstain from

"Breaking or endeavoring to break any blockade lawfully and actually established by or on behalf of either of the said contending parties."

2. The doctrines of blockade, even with the restrictions which have been put upon them, illustrate remarkably the indulgence and partiality exhibited by inter-

---

* *Infra,* p. 84.

national maritime law in favor of belligerents at the expense of neutrals. Two states have a perfect right to go to war with each other on a point the most frivolous imaginable. But are they, or is either of them, entitled to inflict injury, or even serious inconvenience on the rest of mankind, who desire to be at peace? That important question is not discussed by the jurists. Yet it is one very fit for consideration. And here we will enlist the aid of an admirable text, usually, but erroneously attributed to the Roman civil law— a law which has but little in common with the existing code of nations.* *Sic utere tuo, ut alienum non lædas,* which may be thus interpreted: So conduct your war as to inflict no damage on your peaceful neighbors. Now, what is the effect of a blockade? Doubtless, to injure the enemy; and so far, all is fair and right. But suppose it ruins the trade of third parties: suppose it to bring

---

Note as to the Roman Civil Law.

* Those who know the civil law need not be told that it is purely municipal. The modern code of nations considers all states as equal. The Romans admitted no equals. Their "jus gentium" was not international. Let any one find a word about belligerent as contradistinguished from neutral rights in the civil law; or anything about searches for contraband, or breaches of blockade. The Romans, indeed, had a fecial college as old as Numa Pompilius. It ruled forms and ceremonies, but had little to do with justice or humanity. Julius Cæsar, famed for clemency, murdered his prisoners of war. The Iroquois Indians ate theirs; though, as Montesquieu says, they sent and received ambassadors. It was the dismemberment of the Roman empire and the establishment of Christianity, fully developed, that gave birth tardily to the law of nations. It is the opinion of M. Hautefeuille that injudicious attempts to import Roman law into the international, have done harm, the principles of the two systems being essentially different. What is good

starvation on millions of industrious individuals who have nothing to do with the contest but to deplore it, and pray for its cessation. May it not be doubted whether a system which produces the consequences now felt in England and France is not wrong at the foundation? And may it not also be a question whether there is not a time when submission ceases to be a duty, and resistance becomes a virtue? That time, however, we are authorized by high opinions to state, has not yet arrived.*

3. But to resume our exposition. The blockade, to be binding, must be real, and there must be notice of it, so that all to be affected may be upon their guard. The impediment, too, must be by ships of war, placed in such juxtaposition as to enable them to constitute an insuperable barrier. It is said that privateers cannot perform or assist in this work; though

<small>They should be real.</small>

---

in the Roman law is inapplicable; what is bad has done mischief. If Lord Stowell, who made so many prize rulings, once cites a text from the *corpus juris civilis*, on a point of international law, our memory fails. The Rhodians were the true parents of maritime law. Their rules, however, were not international, but municipal, and as such were adopted by Augustus and Antoninus. The truth is that the idea of a code of nations was suggested by the remarkable confederation of the German principalities and the league of free towns, formerly established in different parts of Europe for purposes of mutual protection. See Lord Brougham's Pol. Phil., vol. ii, p. 491; Hallam's Middle Ages, vol. ii, p. 140. Vattel, in his preface, avers that Hobbes was "the first who gave a distinct, but yet imperfect idea of the law of nations;" and this is perhaps the reason why the descendant and editor of that philosopher made the very able speech which will be found *infra*, p. 93.

* Debate in the House of Commons, March 7, 1862; and see, especially, Sir Roundell Palmer's speech, published by Ridgway.

why does not appear, or at all events does not appear rationally.

From these premises it follows that what is called a paper blockade—that is to say, a blockade by mere proclamation, without ships, or with but an inadequate force of ships—is entitled to no deference from neutrals. This doctrine received the sanction of the Paris Congress in 1856.*

4. Then does it follow that a real blockade is harmless? On the contrary, the more impassable the barrier the greater the hardship on innocent sufferers. But a real blockade has limits, which a paper one has not. The real blockade cannot range over three thousand miles of coast. It injures neutrals indeed; but it does not insult their understanding.

The real blockade has limits.

5. It may be said that to abolish blockades would be a hardship upon belligerents. But may it not be answered that to continue blockades would be a greater hardship upon neutrals? Who are the most entitled to favor—the bulk of mankind, who are at peace, or the small, ill-conditioned portion who fight for an idea? Even supposing war to be a necessary evil, the struggle should be to make its mischiefs as small as possible to those not engaged in it.

Ought blockades to be abolished?

6. Breaches of blockade are in the prize court treated as delinquencies, which bring into requisition the criminal vocabulary. Formerly imprisonment or other corpo-

Severe penalties for the breach of them.

---

* See *infra*, pp. 51 and 83.

ral correction, sometimes even death itself,* was inflicted upon offenders. The modern usage has confined the penalty to confiscation of ship and goods. If a vessel has contracted guilt by a breach of blockade, the offence is not discharged till the end of her voyage. But when the blockade itself ceases, the *delictum* ceases. Such is the law as administered in England; and Mr. Justice Story lays down the same doctrine for America.† The decisions for breaches of blockade, though falling short of ancient severity, are still well fitted to secure obedience. Thus, for example, it is held that the mere sailing for a blockaded port, knowing it to be blockaded, is a breach of the blockade, by reason of the criminal intent, which, though unexecuted, involves condemnation.‡

Lord Stowell appears to have considered the breach of a blockade an act of deep turpitude. But it may be doubted whether it would be universally so regarded in the present day. Some might now think it a meritorious achievement, legitimate in object, and not the less entitled to commendation because daring in execution. For, although a breach of blockade is dealt with as a delinquency in the blockading state, it is not so regarded in the neutral state. The Queen's proclamation seems to be but little more than an admonition to her loving subjects, and all who look up to her for protection.§

---

* Manning, 319. † Cranch, p. 440. ‡ 1 Robinson, 154.
§ See Sir Roundell Palmer's speech of the 20th of February, 1862, *infra*, p. 87.

7. In the late dicussion* the solicitor-general made the following remarks as to the essentials of a blockade, having regard to modern changes arising from the use of steam, and other causes.

<small>Essentials of blockade in the present day.</small>

The blockade, says Sir Roundell Palmer,† must be

"A *bona fide* blockade, by a force sufficient to maintain it on the spot; and there must also be a sufficient notification of some kind or other of that blockade. These are the two principles. Whatever may be found in some writers, not now of recent date, it is perfectly clear that we have no exact technical definition of what constitutes such a sufficient force. You cannot *a priori* lay down what particular number of frigates or other ships-of-war shall be an adequate force in any hypothetical case. The improvements in modern warfare, the introduction of steam, or any other similar change, may have made sufficient or insufficient now means of blockade which were not so before."

8. The solicitor-general, on the same occasion, furnished the following test, whereby to fix the sufficiency of a blockade.‡ He said—

<small>Test of sufficiency.</small>

"What, from the beginning of this century, has been laid down as the test in this matter? Why, in the first place, that of 'evident danger;' and then, that due credit must be given to the judgment of the naval officers intrusted with the execution of the service."

9. So, again, as to the intermissions of block-

---

* In the House of Commons, on the 7th of March, 1862.
† Speech of 7th of March, 1862, published by Ridgway.
‡ Ibid.

ade, some inconvenient doctrines are corrected by the solicitor-general in the following passage*— *Intermissions and revivals of blockade.*

"After a blockade has been intermitted, it may be resumed; and when it is resumed, as soon as persons have knowledge of the fact, whether by formal notification of the renewal or otherwise, it becomes as binding again, so far as those persons are concerned, as if it had not been intermitted. It is only during the period of intermission, or as to ships which come in, or intended to come in, during the period of intermission, or which may be affected with notice of the original blockade only, and not of the renewal, that the fact of intermission has any effect."

10. Blockades, like war itself, seem to be a necessity. For this reason it would be desirable, if it were practicable, to render them less noxious to neutrals. What is blockade? Let us look at the plain import of the word. Lord Chancellor Westbury encourages us. He lately resolved, with the concurrence of the other law peers, a most difficult point in the House of Lords, very much by the aid of etymology; which, learnedly and wisely applied, will often clear obscurities, and bring us back to the good sense of a perverted institution. Lord Campbell, on the bench, made many appeals to Dr. Johnson. Now, that great authority tells us that the blockade is simply "to shut up by obstruction." The lexicographer says nothing of seizures or confiscations; because these and the many harsh maxims which attend them have nothing to do with blockade in its primitive and true acceptation. *Blockades without captures.*

---

* Speech of 7th March, 1862, published by Ridgway.

When the first blockader invested a place, he warned off all neutral merchantmen. He "shut them out by obstruction." But it is not clear that he made prizes.

11. We conceive (speaking without experience, having never seen a blockade,) that seizures and confiscations are scarcely worth the trouble, the expense, and the odium they occasion. Whether blockades without captures would prove effective may be a question. But this is to be remembered—the taking of captured ships into port for adjudication is often a tedious and difficult, and sometimes a perilous operation, which must always more or less occasion a diminution of the blockading power, scarcely compensated by the spoil of neutral property, which rewards the men employed.*

<small>Would blockades without captures be effective?</small>

How far this mode of remunerating her majesty's navy is suited to the dignity of a great nation, and how far it comes up to the requirements of an enlightened age, and an advanced civilization, seem to be topics not unfit for the consideration of the legislature.

---

* See *infra*, 42.

Section VII.

The Prize Jurisdiction.

1. Describing the catholic character of the prize jurisdiction, Lord Stowell, at the close of the last century, thus expressed himself— <small>Opinion of Lord Stowell in 1799.</small>

"It is the duty of the judge to administer that justice which the law of nations holds out without distinction to independent states, some happening to be neutral, and some to be belligerent. The seat of judicial authority is indeed locally here, in the belligerent country; but the law itself has no locality. The person who sits here is to determine this question exactly as he would determine the same question if sitting at Stockholm: asserting no pretensions on the part of Great Britain that he would not allow to Sweden."*

2. So said Lord Stowell in 1799. Seven years afterward, France, with hardly a man-of-war at sea, declared England and her colonies in a state of blockade; and England retorted by her orders in council, whereby she declared that France and her allies, as well as her colonies, were in the same predicament. Of course all neutral nations suffered incalculably. They complained that they were made the victims of a double blockade unexampled in its range, yet composed almost entirely of paper, and having not a leg to stand upon in the shape of precedent or authority in the law of nations. They protested without effect. England on the one hand, <small>His opinion in 1812.</small>

---

* 1 Rob. 350.

and the "French Ruler," as he was called, on the other, were too much for the rest of Europe. Still, the neutral traders had one consolation. They called to mind the court which "had its seat locally here, but which was bound to administer a law which had no locality." In answer to their appeal, Lord Stowell "delivered himself with a power of language which never forsook him, and which might have convinced any person except the suffering parties to whom it was addressed." Said this great magistrate, of whom the courts of Doctors' Commons may well be proud—

"It is strictly true that the king in council possesses legislative powers over this court, and may issue orders and instructions which it is bound to obey and enforce: and these constitute the written law of this court. These two propositions, that the court is bound to administer the law of nations, and that it is bound to enforce the king's orders in council, are not at all inconsistent with each other. The constitution of this court relatively to the legislative power of the king in council, is analogous to that of the courts of common law relatively to that of the parliament of this kingdom. Those courts have their unwritten law, the approved principles of natural reason and justice; they have likewise the written or statute law in acts of parliament, which are directory applications of the same principles to particular subjects. What would be the duty of the individuals who preside in those courts, if required to enforce an act of parliament which contradicted those principles, is a question which I presume they would not entertain *a priori*. In like manner, this court will not let itself loose into speculations as to what would be its duty under such an emergency, because it cannot, without extreme indecency, presume that any such emergency will happen."

3. The discerning reader will perhaps recognize

the hand that penned the following paragraph*— *These opinions contrasted.*

"If we venture to dispute the law recently laid down by the learned judge (Lord Stowell), it is upon his own authority. By what stretch of ingenuity can we reconcile the position that the court treats the English government and foreign governments alike, determining the cause exactly as it would if sitting in the claimant's country, with the new position that the English government possesses legislative powers over the court, and that its orders are, in the law of nations, what statutes are in the municipal law?"

4. The result is that our prize court, while affecting to administer the maritime law of nations, is in fact bound to obey orders in council, and proclamations issued by one of the very parties who are litigating before it. *The court has two masters.*

5. On this point we consider it a positive duty to quote the following admirable sentences from the skilful pen aforesaid†— *Serious consequence.*

"What analogy is there between the proclamations of one belligerent as relating to points in the law of nations, and the enactments of statute as regarding the common law of the land? Were there indeed any general council of civilized states — any congress such as that fancied in Henry IV's famous project for a perpetual peace — any Amphyctyonic council for modern Europe, its decisions and edicts might bear to the established public law the same relation that statutes have to the municipal code; because they would be the enactments of a common head, binding on and acknowledged by the whole body. But the edicts of one state, in questions between that state and foreign powers — or between that state and the subjects of foreign powers — or between those who stand in the place of that state

---

* *Edinb. Rev.*, Feb., 1812.   † Ibid.

and foreign governments or individuals—much more nearly resemble the acts of a party to the cause than the enactments of the law by which both parties are bound to abide. Mark the consequences of such loose doctrines, such feeble analogies. They resolve themselves into an immediate denial that any such thing as the law of nations exists, or that contending parties have any common court to which all may resort for justice. There may be a court for French captors in France, and for English captors in England. To these tribunals such parties may respectively appeal in safety: for they derive their rights from edicts issued by the governments of the two countries severally; and those edicts are good law in the prize courts of each. But for the American neutral claimant there is no law by which he may be redressed; no court to which he may resort. He is a prey to the orders of each belligerent in succession. Even under the old and pure system of 1798 and 1799, the neutral was forced to receive his sentence in a foreign court, always the court of the captor's country. But how is it now, when the court, sitting as before, has made so large a stride in allegiance as to profess an implicit obedience to the orders of the belligerent government within whose dominions it acts?"

6. Dr. Phillimore is clear that the "orders in council of 1807 contravened the international law;" but he admits that Lord Stowell "carried them into execution."*

<small>Lord Stowell's position difficult.</small>

The position of this judge was one of difficulty. He acted under two authorities. He tried to obey both, even when they disagreed. We can now do justice to his motives; but his fine diction, his delightful manners,† and his real purity all failed to save him from the censure of his contemporaries. Thus, in addition to the strictures we have quoted, we find that Mr. Horner, who was in constant communication with some of the best

---

* 3 Phill. Int. Law, p. 539.   † See Townsend's Memoir.

men of his time (among others, Sir Samuel Romilly, Sir James Macintosh, and Lord Henry Petty), wrote to John Allen:* "Sir William Scott (Lord Stowell) is said to have furnished ministers with his opinion in favor of our right to search ships-of-war for deserters." The British government had the very month before conveyed to the American minister a disavowal of any such right.† About the same period,‡ Mr. Horner, writing to Mr. Murray (afterward the eminent Scotch judge), says: "Sir William Scott told Sydney Smith that no *principle* is more *plainly* laid down than our right to take the navy of the Danes; and so he has been ready to say, and would be still ready, for any outrage or breach of the law of nations that the government of this country has dared or is meditating to commit." The remarks of Mr. Horner are too severe; but they show the impression entertained respecting Lord Stowell by men of the first eminence in this country. But if we turn to foreign witers of neutral nations we shall find not only strong reprehension, but even imputations of corruption. The American jurist, Mr. Wheaton, who had served diplomatically in sundry parts of Europe, sets out in his "Elements" the grievances of the Baltic powers, which they referred to the supposed "tyranny" of England, as exercised in her prize jurisdiction. He goes particularly into the complaints of Denmark, when Lord Stowell decided that ships

---

* August 31, 1807. Horner's Memoirs.
† See 4 James' Nav. Hist., 333.   ‡ September 29, 1807.

under convoy were liable to visit and search, and subject to confiscation for refusing to submit to either.* Mr. Wheaton was himself deeply imbued with the feelings described by him. Speaking of Lord Stowell, he says, "that highly gifted and accomplished man has been compelled to avow that he was bound by the king's instructions; and we know that his decrees are liable to be reversed by the privy council, from which those instructions emanate. The rapacity and injustice of the British courts of vice-admiralty in the colonies are notorious."† Mr. Wheaton even talks of "the pure hands" of the American judges,‡ apparently by way of contrast to the hands of Lord Stowell, and the hands of the colonial vice-admiralty judges. The editor of the "Elements," Mr. Lawrence, charges Lord Stowell with "ministerial subserviency."§ He remarks that Lord Stowell "at one time appeared to regard the text of the king's instructions as binding on his conscience; at another, he held it indecorous to anticipate the possibility of their conflicting with the law of nations."|| It is very

---

* *Maria*, 1 Robinson, 340. Lord Stowell's judgment in this case is admirable in composition, argument, and diction; but the decision is in the last degree questionable. Mr. Massey, in his instructive history, says, "a right of search can never be made to extend to ships under the immediate protection of a man-of-war. An attempt to enforce it under such circumstances is an insult to the flag so challenged." It is curious that Lord Stowell, in this case, speaks about the Roman civil law; but he cites no text, and we believe it would be difficult to find one, on the privileges of maritime convoy.

† Introd. Rem., 37. § Introd. Rem., 79.
‡ Ibid. || Ibid.

true the same writers are equally liberal of their condemnation when speaking of French prize jurisdictions. But this only raises these questions: first, whether neutrals are likely ever to be satisfied with adjudications coming from a belligerent state, their opponent in the prize litigation; and secondly, whether it would not be better to place this invidious jurisdiction in some separate, independent, and disinterested territory. This suggestion, however, is not free from difficulties; nor are we at all clear that any good would come of it. It is the law itself—so hard on neutrals—that causes the evil, and not the instrument of its administration.

7. It is not wonderful that Lord Stowell should have been considered a harsh judge toward neutrals; for unless where there was gross culpability on the part of the captors, although restitution might be ultimately ordered, neither damages nor costs were awarded against them.

<small>Lord Stowell severe on neutrals.</small>

8. We are told by that eminent judge, Dr. Lushington, that, "during the seventeen years Lord Stowell presided in the prize court he had condemned captors in costs and damages in only about ten or a dozen cases; not one in a thousand."* On another occasion Dr. Lushington said "he believed that not one case would be found where Lord Stowell condemned the captors in costs and damages upon the ground

<small>Indulgent to captors.</small>

---

* The *Ostsee*, Dr. Spinks' Prize Cases, 174.

that the papers and depositions did not disclose a probable cause of capture."* Accordingly, the marginal note or summary of a most important case decided by Dr. Lushington during the late Russian war is in these words: "If captors seize a vessel without any ostensible cause, they are liable to costs and damages; but this is the extremity of the law of nations, and should only be adopted in cases of imperative necessity."† Such cases were evidently rare in Lord Stowell's time; though not quite so rare as Dr. Lushington imagined; for on an appeal from his decision in "The *Ostsee*," coming before the Judicial Committee, in 1856, Lord Kingsdown, in giving judgment, observed "that the cases in which during the late war restitution was attended with costs and damages turn out upon inquiry to be more numerous than was supposed."‡

9. In those cases, undoubtedly few and far between, where damages and costs were awarded against the captors, the amount was generally, if not invariably, made good by the government. And this was not unreasonable. It was the policy of the government to stimulate the energy of its officers; and if they acted in obedience to orders, the state must indemnify them. It appears, accordingly, that the occupation of captors was not without other advantages besides the satisfaction which arises from

Prize money awarded to captors.

---

* The *Leucade*, Spinks' Prize Cases, 224.
† The *Ostsee*, Dr. Spinks' Rep., 174.
‡ Spinks' Prize Cases, 174.

the performance of a duty—the general practice having been to distribute among them the proceeds of prizes,* *pour encourager les autres.*† The practice in America appears to correspond; for we remark that Captain Wilkes claimed credit for the sacrifice he made in forbearing to take the *Trent* into port on a late memorable occasion.‡

10. It requires but little reflection to perceive that random seizures must have been frequent under a system which rewarded the captors with prize money when in the right, and protected them from penalties when in the wrong. Lord Kingsdown has said "that the temptation to send in ships for adjudication is sufficiently strong." In Lord Stowell's time it was too strong. Temptations to random captures.

11. The law of Lord Stowell bound his successor, Dr. Lushington, in the court below; but it was corrected in the judicial committee by Lord Kingsdown, from whose judgment we deduce the following propositions— Correction of Lord Stowell's law.

---

* 3 Phillimore, Int. Law, 459.

† A most learned friend states, with reference to the practice in Lord Stowell's time, that the desire of encouraging captures was predominant. The distinction, however, was made between the captors, whether they were officers in the navy or captains of privateers. In the case of the former, the court 'felt great anxiety to protect them, perhaps sometimes even beyond what could be strictly reconciled with principle.' *Nemesis*, Edw. Rep., 52. At all events, except in flagrant cases, it would protect them. Upon several, besides those referred to in 'the *Ostsee*,' the court has intimated an opinion that the government should protect officers in the navy."

‡ See his letter to the Secretary of the Navy at New York, dated from on board the *San Jacinto*, at sea, November 16, 1861.

- 4

"A ship may by her own misconduct have occasioned her capture; and in such a case it is very reasonable that she should indemnify the captors against the expenses which her misconduct has occasioned.

"Or, she may be involved, with little or no fault on her part, in such suspicion as to make it the right, or even the duty of a belligerent to seize her. There may be no fault either in the captor or the captured; or both may be in fault; and in such cases there may be *damnum absque injuria*, and no ground for anything but simple restitution.

"Or there may be a third case, where not only the ship is in no fault, but she is not, by any act of her own, voluntary or involuntary, open to any fair ground of suspicion. In such a case a belligerent may seize at his peril, and take the chance of something appearing on investigation to justify the capture; but if he fails in such a case it seems very fit that he should pay the costs and damages which he has occasioned."*

Section VIII.

Late Changes in the Maritime Law of Nations.

1. At the close of the Crimean war the leading powers of Europe, namely, Great Britain, Austria, France, Russia, Prussia, Sardinia, and Turkey were represented at Paris by their respective plenipotentiaries, who, assembled in congress, applied themselves to the important task of amending what they call the "maritime law in time of war;" that law having long been confessedly productive of "deplorable disputes," which, they held, might thereafter "occasion serious difficulties, and even conflicts." To

<small>The Paris "solemn declarations."</small>

---

* 2 Spinks' Ecc. and Adm. Rep., 171.

avert such calamities for the future the plenipotentiaries, on the 16th April, 1856, "adopted" certain "solemn declarations," which will in due time be specified.

2. But before doing so it is fit that we consider for a moment how far these "solemn declarations" are binding. On this interesting point Lord Derby* has made the following observations — *(How far they bind.)*

" Undoubtedly, it is true, that the agreement of the congress has not up to the present moment the binding force of a treaty, nor has it been ratified by the sovereign. It does not alter the real state of international law ; but I hold that all the powers whose representatives signed this paper, and who have not since disavowed it, are morally bound by the liabilities and obligations imposed upon them at the time."

If this country is morally bound, it is bound legally; for although there is some countenance for the doctrine which says that an engagement entered into by a plenipotentiary requires the subsequent ratification of the sovereign, yet is this a doctrine which most people will think more honored in the breach than the observance; and such evidently is the opinion of Lord Derby. It is also the opinion of Lord Russell, who, though he holds that the "declarations" were on our part "very imprudent," and though he considers the "whole matter most unsatisfactory," he yet "does not see that a breach of faith would at all mend our position."†

---

* 7th Feb., 1862.

† *Hansard*, July 14, 1857. It appears that the Paris declarations are now agreed to by all the great states except America.

We have, moreover, the reply of Lord Granville to Lord Derby, stating that the course taken by our plenipotentiary* had the entire approbation of the British government, who, after many interchanges of communication, and after profound deliberation, came to be of a clear opinion "that it was for the benefit of this country that the rules agreed upon at Paris should be adopted."

3. This being so, let us examine the "solemn declarations" in their order. The first of them is couched with commendable brevity in the following odd terms —

<small>Privateering abolished.</small>

Privateering is and remains abolished.

Great Britain is supposed to have gained much by the abolition of privateering. The French journalists allege that it was for this reason she acceded to the second "solemn declaration," which we shall come to presently. In fact, Lord Clarendon has said as much. On the 22d May, 1856, in his place in the House of Lords, giving an account of his stewardship at Paris, he, among other things, stated that the abolition of privateering was "more than an equivalent for the abandonment of a claim which could not have been sustained."

4. America was asked to concur with the plenipotentiaries, but she refused, simply because America wished to retain privateering, unless a resolution were come to that all private property, belligerent as well as neutral, should be held inviolable and sacred at sea. Both

<small>Effect on America.</small>

---

* The Earl of Clarendon.

countries, England and America, proceeded on intelligible principles. England has a great mercantile marine, and also a great navy. She therefore requires no privateers, and it is her interest that other nations should dispense with them. America, on the other hand, has a great mercantile marine, but a small navy. America consequently encourages individual enterprise in war, and is in fact obliged to rely upon it. The legislature of New York, in 1812, passed an act to promote privateering associations, to whom corporate privileges were given for the purpose, as Chancellor Kent tells us, of "annoying the enemy, and injuring their commerce."* It may be said, and with great probability, that hostilities conducted by buccaneering companies are not likely to furnish edifying examples of forbearance. But they can only plunder, and imitate successfully her majesty's cruisers. Both are stimulated by booty. The comparative degrees of eagerness we need not investigate.

The Paris declaration binds only those who were parties to it. It therefore does not bind the Americans; neither would it bind this country in a war with them.

5. The second "solemn declaration," the most important of all, was a prodigious advance in maritime law reform. The ancient *Consolato del Mare* had declared more than six centuries ago that merchandise

Enemy's goods safe under neutral flag.

---

* 1 Comm. 98.

belonging to an enemy was confiscable, though found in the ship of a friend. This harsh rule, unless qualified by treaty, was invariably enforced by the English prize court, though it was not always followed by the Continental states. But it has been reversed and extinguished by the congress of Paris. The change is pronounced by M. Hautefeuille to be a mighty triumph of civilization over what he calls the "ferocious maxims of the middle ages"; and it is thus justified by Lord Clarendon—

"In the course of the last two centuries, one hundred and thirty international engagements have been made between the principal powers of the world, in all of which, with eleven exceptions, the rule, "free ships, free goods," is contained. What I deduce from this is, that in time of war, and in the heat and animosity of war, men lay aside this principle, and resort to extreme and violent measures; but that when at peace, and under the influence of reason and judgment, they never hesitate to declare that that should be the rule of civilized nations."

Every other maritime power in the world has protested against our practice, and at the commencement of the Russian war England was the only power which upheld the right of seizure.*

The words which have introduced this important revolution are the following—

The neutral flag covers enemy's goods, with the exception of contraband of war.

A death-blow is here given to the authority of many valued judgments of the prize court, and

---

* Hansard, 22d May, 1856.

many cherished doctrines of the jurist, which are wholly swept away if we suppose the second "solemn declaration" to be binding.

6. Lord Derby has serious misgivings as to the wording of the second "solemn declaration." He thus expresses his apprehensions— *Lord Derby's apprehensions.*

"I confess that I regret—and I expressed my regret at the time*—the sacrifice which, as I thought, my noble friend† had made in 1856, when he consented, on the part of the government of this country, to the principle that enemy's goods should be safe on board neutral vessels. I thought this a dangerous concession for a country situated as ours is; and I remonstrated against it."‡

7. Lord Palmerston, on the other hand, forebodes no evil from what was done at Paris. According to his lordship, "the idea that the results of war depend upon *Lord Palmerston's good auguries.* the capture of an enemy's goods on board of neutral bottoms can only originate in a mind wholly unacquainted with the most familiar lessons of history."§ Alluding to the fact that Queen Victoria had, at the beginning of the Russian war, in March, 1854,‖ waived her right to seize enemy's goods in neutral vessels, Lord Palmerston, in his Liverpool speech, on the 7th November, 1856, stated that while the effect of the waiver was not "in any degree to impair the power of the belligerents against their opponents, it yet tended to

---

* Hansard, 22d May, 1856. § *Star*, 6th Feb., 1862.
† Lord Clarendon. ‖ *Infra*, p. 92.
‡ *Times*, 7th Feb. 1862.

mitigate the pressure which hostilities inevitably produced upon the commercial transactions of countries that were at war."*

8. The following imaginary but trying case was put on the 7th February, 1862, by Lord Derby—

Case put by Lord Derby.

"If we had gone to war with the Federal States, I will ask, in passing, what would have been the result of our adoption of the doctrines of the congress? We had an agreement—I won't call it a convention—with France. We had no agreement with America. In the event of a war with America, therefore, American merchandise on board a French vessel would, by our obligations with France, be safe against our cruisers; and American commerce would enjoy impunity when carried on in French vessels, owing to an agreement in which America had no part. Thus the treaty would have a very one-sided operation, and one nation would secure all the benefits without being a party to it, while the other would sacrifice all its advantages, because she *was* a party to it. That is a position in which England ought not to stand toward any country whatever."†

9. Earl Granville replied by showing the course which Great Britain would take under the new regime. His lordship said—

Answer by Lord Granville.

"I think the noble earl was not quite right in the illustration he gave of the effect of allowing neutral ships to carry the goods of belligerents. If a war arose with the United States, I have no doubt that our first operation would be to blockade, and that in a very efficient manner, all the ports of that country, thereby putting a considerable and speedy check upon the American trade. And so far from its being a disadvantage that any commerce which she carried on should be carried on in neutral bottoms, it would be quite the reverse."

---

* *Times*, 8th November, 1856.   † *Times*, 7th Feb., 1862.

10. The third "solemn declaration" of the Paris congress is that— *Neutral goods safe under enemy's flag.*
Neutral goods, with the exception of contraband of war, are not liable to capture under enemy's flag.

Here no change is introduced so far as this country is concerned; for it was ever the English and American practice to respect neutral property in hostile ships. The ships indeed were captured, but the goods of the friendly owner were uniformly surrendered to him. In this respect the practice of some Continental states differed from our own; but the difference is only matter of history, and need not be gone into, the new jurisprudence of Europe on the high seas now being that the neutral flag protects an enemy's property; and that neutral property is safe, though found under an enemy's flag.

11. We now come to the fourth and last "solemn declaration" of the plenipotentiaries, namely, that— *What blockades bind by the Paris declaration.*
Blockades in order to be binding must be effective—that is to say, maintained by a force sufficient really to prevent access to the coast of the enemy.

On the subject of blockades we have already said enough.* The "solemn declaration" does alter the law as laid down by approved authorities.

12. The Queen's proclamation† charges her subjects to abstain from "breaking, or endeavoring to break, any blockade, lawfully and actually established by, or on *Variance by Queen's proclamation.*

---

* See *supra*, p. 27.   † *Infra*, p. 84.

behalf of the contending parties; but it does not say that such blockade "must be effective—that is to say, maintained by a force sufficient really to prevent access to the coasts of the enemy."

This variance is not likely to have been accidental. Those who drew up the Queen's proclamation must have had before them at the time the Paris declaration. The deviation, therefore, was by design and for a purpose—possibly the laudable one of adhering to precedents: seeing that America was no party to the Paris declarations. Foreign critics, however, resort to a less charitable construction; for they more than insinuate that the effective blockades described by the plenipotentiaries are viewed with disfavor by the British government.

Section IX.

Proposed Changes in the Maritime Law of Nations.

1. After the great step taken by the Paris plenipotentiaries, in 1856, the question remains—an important and a difficult one—whether a further stride in the same direction has not become expedient; in other words, whether it is not fit to put an end at once to the practice which, as has been shown, prevails during war, of attacking and plundering the property of private individuals at sea. Some think a change in this respect imperative; others hold it would be dangerous. On what

<small>Ought private property to be respected at sea?</small>

principle are we to proceed—the good of England, or of the world at large? Is it clear that they differ? The eye of the publicist looks to the great family of nations, having regard to what is best for mankind. The municipal lawyer thinks of nothing but the interests of his own country. The statesman must decide.

If wars could be prevented or arranged by arbitration,* the gain would be immeasurable; but before any hope of such happy results can be relied upon, human nature, we fear, must undergo a change, of which the indications as yet are only partial and feeble, if not hollow and deceitful. Therefore it is, that a strong effort should be made

---

* The Paris plenipotentiaries received with great favor a suggestion much urged by Lord Clarendon, that friendly mediation ought in all cases to be resorted to before commencing hostilities. This appears by the protocol of the 14th April, 1856, from which we extract the following passages: *Protocol as to mediation to prevent war.*

"The Earl of Clarendon having demanded permission to lay before the congress a proposition which it appeared to him ought to be favorably received, stated that the calamities of war were still too present to every mind not to make it desirable to seek out every expedient calculated to prevent their return; that a stipulation had been inserted in article vii, of the treaty of peace (of 1856), recommending that in case of difference between the Porte and one or more of the other signing powers, recourse should be had to the mediation of a friendly state before resorting to force. The first plenipotentiary of Great Britain conceived that this happy innovation might receive a more general application, and thus become a barrier against conflicts which frequently only break forth because it is not always possible to enter into explanation, and to come to an understanding. He proposed, therefore, to agree upon a resolution calculated to afford to the maintenance of peace that chance of duration hereafter, without prejudice, however, to the independence of governments. Count Walewski declared himself authorized to support the idea expressed by the first plenipotentiary of Great Britain; he gave the assurance that the plenipotentiaries of

to render an evil so difficult to avert as contracted in the range of its mischiefs as possible.

2. Now it has been said, and said with plausibility, that war ought to be the affair of governments, not of individuals, nor even of nations. We presume that this was Lord Palmerston's meaning when he said at Liverpool that "it was, perhaps, to be desired that conflicts should be confined to the bodies acting under the orders and directions of the respective states."* On one occasion the distinction between an armed enemy and a pacific trader was mutually guaranteed by treaty; a treaty which on this account deserves honorable mention—

America always for immunity.

France were wholly disposed to concur in the insertion in the protocol of a wish which, being fully in accordance with the tendencies of our epoch, would not in any way fetter the free action of governments. The Earl of Clarendon replied that each power is, and will be the sole judge of the requirements of its honor and its interests; that it was by no means his intention to restrict the authority of the governments, but only to afford them the opportunity of not having recourse to arms whenever differences might be adjusted by other means. The wish of the congress should allow of the most general application; be observed that if the good offices of another power had induced the government of Greece to respect the laws of neutrality, France and England would very probably have abstained from occupying the Piræus with their troops. He referred to the efforts made by the Cabinet of Great Britain in 1823, in order to prevent the armed intervention which took place at that time in Spain. Whereupon the plenipotentiaries did not hesitate to express, in the name of their governments, the wish that states between which any serious misunderstanding may arise should, before appealing to arms, have recourse, as far as circumstances might allow, to the good offices of a friendly power.

"The plenipotentiaries hoped that the governments not represented at the congress would unite in the sentiment which had inspired the wish recorded in the present protocol."

* *Times*, 8th November, 1856.

that between America and Prussia in 1785.* And here we must remember that the Americans, ever since the declaration of their independence, and more especially since the commencement of the war of 1793, have uniformly insisted "that public ships should not capture any merchant vessels, or otherwise plunder private property upon the ocean; but confine their belligerent operations exclusively to the ships of war of each nation."† It appears, indeed, that so recently as June, 1861, the minister of the United States at Paris proposed to the French government "to add to the first article of the declaration of 1856 the plan of protecting private property on the sea from capture in time of war."‡ How far this is practicable, how far it is wise, must soon be decided. It is, at all events, opposed by the jurists, who hold that the very notion of war necessarily implies a cessation of all commercial intercourse between the belligerents.

3. The first Napoleon, a man of speculation as well as of practice, dissented from the jurists. He held that "belligerents ought to wage war without giving rise to the confiscation of their mercantile marine. Commerce should be

Opinion of Napoleon I.

---

* During war certain favored persons are authorized to trade with the enemy. Others do so without license—by connivance. This shows that convenience is felt from the practice on both sides; and it would rather appear that there is but little wisdom in restricting it.

† Rush's Residence at the Court of London. Sec. Ser., vol. ii, p. 121.

‡ Correspondence respecting International Maritime Law. North America, No. 3. Presented to Parliament, 1862, p. 7.

carried on by sea between the two belligerents as it is carried on by land in the midst of the battles of the contending parties."*

4. So, Lord Palmerston, no enthusiastic innovator, addressing the Liverpool chamber of commerce, on the 7th November, 1856, said: "It has been a subject of great satisfaction to us† to reflect that at the commencement of the Russian conflict the government of England, in concert with that of France, made changes and relaxations in the doctrines of war which, without in any degree impairing the power of the belligerents against their opponents, maintained the course of hostilities, yet tended to mitigate the pressure which hostilities inevitably produce upon the commercial transactions of countries that are at war. I cannot help hoping that those relaxations of former doctrines which were established in the beginning of the war, practised during its continuance, and which have been since ratified by formal engagements, *may perhaps be still further extended;* and in the course of time those principles of war which are applied to hostilities by land may be extended, without exception, to hostilities by sea; so that private property shall no longer be the object of aggression on either side. If we look at the example of former periods we shall not find that any powerful country was ever vanquished through the losses of individuals. It is

Of Lord Palmerston.

---

* Quoted by Mr. Lindsay in a letter to Earl Russell.
† His lordship was then, as now, Chief Minister.

the conflict of armies by land, and of fleets by sea, that decides the great contests of nations."* It took the Saxons one hundred and fifty years of murderous and devastating raids to establish themselves in this island. One pitched battle, that of Hastings, completed the Norman conquest in a day.

5. The country which has the greatest naval force has also the greatest trade, and the largest amount of property afloat. Consequently the losses of that nation may, peradventure, be greater than her captures, regard being had to the difficulty which the most effective navy will experience in protecting countless merchantmen on every sea. This difficulty will be increased if we suppose the country to be at any time in danger of invasion, and the navy to be required for the protection of her coasts. It may therefore be the policy of that nation to join in establishing a universal immunity for merchant ships and their cargoes, whether neutral or belligerent, during hostilities, so as to save them at once from the depredations of cruisers, and the obstructions of blockades. If, however, blockades were reconcilable with the universal immunity desired by merchants and ship-owners, then England would be safe, for she could blockade her enemy's ports so as to destroy his trade, while at the same time her own commerce might proceed without interruption.†

_{What the policy of Great Britain.}

---

* *Times*. 8th November, 1856.
† See *Saturday Review*, March 15, 1862. But see the remarks of Sir R. Palmer, *infra*, p. 78.

6. Judging from the resolutions of chambers of commerce, and from the evidence taken before the shipping committee,* it is plain that the mercantile body desire this large immunity. Mr. A. Gilmour is "for doing away with captures entirely." Mr. S. R. Graves "sees no reason why private property should be confiscated at sea, and on land allowed to go free." He holds that "England's commerce has become so large that she cannot protect it." Mr. A. Anderson is of opinion that "it would be very desirable if England could make a step further in advance, and proclaim that all private property should be exempt from-capture at sea." Mr. T. E. Smith thinks "it would be very desirable if we could get all private property exempted from capture in case of war." And Mr. J. Beazley is still more emphatic, for he says: "Do away with the right of capture, or ruin our British shipping —one or the other."†

Opinion of the mercantile body.

7. The question, however, is not to be decided by merchants and ship-owners. We have the report of a committee of the House of Commons,‡ who affirm that— .

Report of Commons' Committee.

"Though grave objections have been urged by high authorities against any further step in advance, they (the committee) are of opinion that in the progress of civilization, and in the

---

* House of Commons, session 1860.

† Report of Commons' Committee on Shipping, 1860.

‡ There were on this committee, besides very eminent merchants (including Mr. Baring), two cabinet ministers, Mr. Milner Gibson and Mr. Cardwell; and also Lord Lovaine.

cause of humanity, the time has arrived when all private property, not contraband of war, should be exempt from capture at sea; and Great Britain is deeply interested in the adoption of this course."

8. The Secretary of State for foreign affairs, having been asked, on the 18th February, 1861, whether any steps had been taken by the government to carry out the recommendations of the shipping committee, gave an answer which shows that Earl Russell, though a reformer, pauses a little before adopting a principle which may be found in practice less beneficial to this country than acceptable to others. His lordship treats the committee's proposition as somewhat Utopian. He says — Opinion of Earl Russell.

"The proposition itself seems to me to be one of the utmost magnitude. It is, in fact, a proposal, that, there being two powers, one of which has a very strong army and a weak navy—the other having an army inferior in numbers, but a superior navy—the power which has the superior navy should forego all the advantage to be derived from that source, and allow the contest to be decided by military force alone. Its adoption would in the next place tend rather to prolong than to shorten wars; because one way in which a great maritime power can act as a belligerent, is to cripple the trade of its opponent. The greater its strength as a maritime power, the greater is its power to do this, and the better its chance of bringing the war to a favorable termination. If this proposition were accepted, the whole of the power would be gone which has hitherto rendered Great Britain so formidable at sea. In the next place, I perceive difficulties in detail which would be insurmountable. The mercantile navy of a belligerent would be free from capture; but no one could say, when a number of vessels, apparently merchant ships, appeared off the coast, that they might not be used for purposes of war, and that they did not contain ———

[Here his lordship was interrupted by Mr. Bright, but on resuming, said —] I regard the question as one affecting the whole maritime power of this country. And I think that any minister of the crown ought to be most cautious in taking any final step in respect of it."

These considerations are truly serious. The subject calls for greatly more discussion than it has hitherto received. The legislature has not examined it; and the press has not yet sufficiently aroused to it the attention of the country.

9. I believe I have now done fairly what I proposed at the outset, which was, to state shortly the chief points — to offer here and there a suggestion — and to leave to the reader's judgment the decision.

Conclusion.

Section X.

Postscript.

Showing the Present State of Sentiment in the House of Commons as to Securing an Immunity for all Private Property at Sea during Hostilities.*

On the 11th of March, 1862, Mr. Horsfall † called the attention of the House of Commons to the subject of international maritime law, and moved a resolution that the existing state of that law as "affecting belligerents and neutrals was unsatisfactory, and called for the early attention of the government." The real object of the motion was to obtain a discussion of the subject. After describing the old law, and the changes made at Paris in 1856, the honorable member stated his own view to be that all private property during war should be inviolable at sea —

Mr. Horsfall's motion to abolish mercantile captures.

"The question was, first, what would be the effect of the law in the event of war; and, secondly, what had been its effect in time of peace. Merchants would not

His opinion.

---

* The speeches which follow are abridged from the *Times* of 12th and 17th of March, 1862.

† Member for Liverpool.

ship a single package of goods in a vessel liable to seizure if they had the opportunity of shipment in a vessel not so liable.

<small>Evil of the law in war.</small>
The operation of the law in the event of a war, say with France, would be that every British ship would be laid by. Neutral vessels would obtain greatly enhanced freights; and British seamen would be drafted from British ships not into her majesty's navy, but into neutral vessels that could afford to pay much higher wages than had ever been or ever could be paid in our navy. This was a most serious matter for the ship-owner, the manufacturer, and the country at large.

<small>In peace.</small>
But what had been the effect of the law in time of peace? On the mere rumor of war a second-class American vessel was able to get freights at a 50 per cent. higher rate than a first-class British ship could obtain. English merchants were so afraid to ship their tea in British ships that they shipped in American vessels—these not being subject to capture. We must either go back, or we must go forward. In case of war, ships would require a convoy. That convoy would be much better employed in fighting the enemy. Her majesty had declared her anxiety to 'lessen as much as possible the evils of war.' The most difficult part of the question was the subject of blockade.

<small>Difficulty as to blockade.</small>
Those whom he represented were in favor of respecting the blockade of the Southern ports. As to privateering great injustice had been done to the Americans. They would not give it up unless the great powers of Europe would consent to take the still wider ground that all private property should be free. He asked the House to adopt his motion; and he did so in the name of the commerce of the country, and of civilization, humanity, and justice."

The Attorney-General* addressed the House in an able speech, but rather with the view of expounding and vindicating the law as it now stands than of discussing the merits of the changes proposed, or the effect which

<small>The Attorney-General's opinion.</small>

---

* Sir William Atherton.

they were likely to produce on the general interests of the country. He held that the declaration of Paris was a concluded fact. *Paris declaration final.*

Mr. Liddell* denied that the importance of this subject was confined to the shipping interest— *Mr. Liddell's opinion.*

"The doctrine which lay at the root of our present maritime law was that a strong belligerent should by means of its supremacy at sea harass and weaken the enemy. But by admitting foreigners to our colonial and coasting trade we had rendered it impossible for us in future to act upon that principle, without in time of war handing over the whole of our commerce to the ships of other countries. For these reasons we must recognize and forward the principle of granting immunity to private property at sea. We should invite a congress to promote the general progress of commerce, and to consider how best to protect the property of unoffending ship-owners from rapine and destruction." *We should support immunity.*

Mr. Baillie Cochrane† censured the declaration of Paris as a great blunder. But he should regard the adoption of the motion before the House as a still more unfortunate event. *Mr. Baillie Cochrane's opinion. Paris declaration a blunder.*

Sir George Bowyer‡ said it was difficult to understand why the analogy of terrestrial war should not prevail with respect to war at sea. A belligerent had no more right to seize a merchant's ship on the sea than he had to seize the property of the people whom he invaded by land. *Sir George Bowyer's opinion. Analogy between sea and land warfare.*

---

* Member for S. Northumberland.
† Member for Honiton.   ‡ Member for Dundalk.

Sir George C. Lewis* said the question was of first-rate importance; and it was of paramount importance that it should receive a right decision in that house—

Sir George C. Lewis' opinion.

"Neutrals have no interest in the principle which the honorable mover recommends to the house. Neutrals, so far as they had any interest, had an interest directly opposite, because if they wished to become the carriers of the world they would naturally wish that the ships and goods of the belligerents should be exposed to risk. You may make a compact that in time of war you will respect the neutral flag. For instance, we have now a compact with France and other Continental powers that we will act on the principle that the neutral flag covers the enemy's goods, so that if we were to seize American goods under the French flag we should be guilty of a violation of engagement with France. But war puts an end to all treaties and engagements in the nature of a treaty. Therefore if we had unfortunately found ourselves involved in hostilities with the United States, and if we had previously had a treaty with the United States recognizing the principle that belligerents were to spare one another's mercantile marine, the very act of war would have put an end to that treaty, and it would have been in the discretion of either power whether or no they would act on that principle. It is an absurdity to suppose that if we were at war with France or Russia the declaration of Paris would have any binding effect upon us except in regard to our honor. It is not binding by international law. If the United States of America approve so highly of the principle of not capturing enemy's ships and goods, why don't they establish that principle with respect to the Southern states? Here is a fine opportunity for the government of Washington acting on that principle. No doubt it is said the Southerners are rebels; but in the exchange of prisoners, and in the matter of blockades, they

Neutrals opposed to the motion.

War puts an end to treaties.†

---

* Secretary of State for the Department of War.
† Wheaton's Elements, 340.

have been treated in all respects as belligerents. If that be the case, why does not the government of Washington show its forbearance in not capturing enemy's goods? It is said that all private property is spared in land warfare. I must meet that assertion by a most formal denial. I say that by the laws of land warfare, as recognized by the most civilized nations, and according to the most recent practice, private property is not respected except so far as suits the present convenience of the belligerent armies.* When you conquer a country you conquer its government; and when you have conquered its government you have conquered that agent by which the country can be plundered: Perhaps this language might be somewhat homely; nevertheless it expressed the exact truth. With regard to the sea there was no similar engine; and the only way in which a belligerent could exercise any control over property at sea was by capture. The real analogy between land and sea warfare was effected by the declaration of Paris when this country abolished privateering. We do not permit a single private individual to go out on a plundering expedition. At the same time we do not restrain the army from seizing private property whenever such seizure may be necessary. With our fleet at Portsmouth or Plymouth, to allow enemy's ships to go in and out free from capture seemed to be carrying the doctrine of forbearance in time of war to an absurd point."

Property not spared on land.

Mr. T. Baring had listened with some surprise to the speech of the right honorable gentleman the Secretary for War (Sir George Lewis), who had said that no compact or treaty made during peace was binding in war.

Mr. T. Baring's opinion.

Sir G. C. Lewis (interrupting) said —

Sir G. C. Lewis' explanation.

"This is so important a point that I should be sorry if any misunderstanding arose. What I meant

---

* Here the right honorable gentleman gave an account of the Duke of Wellington's proceedings in Spain — not a hostile country, but a country we were assisting.

to say, and what I believe I did say was, that I conceived the declaration of Paris to be binding as between this country and neutrals during the existence of war; and to be equally binding with a treaty, though it was only a declaration; but that if we were at war with any of the parties to that declaration, then, like other treaties, it would cease to have a binding effect as regards that belligerent."

Mr. Baring's opinion. Mr. Baring resumed, and made the following observations —

"The attorney-general had treated the Paris declaration as an accomplished fact, which must be adhered to. In *Paris declaration binding.* the case of a war between this country and France, is it not evident that the whole of your carrying-trade would pass into the hands of neutrals? What country has most commerce afloat? most property to be seized? Surely, England. What country would gain most by the preservation of that property? England. What country would be so much injured in war, through her commerce, as England? There is not the slightest doubt that you ought gravely to consider the motion before us. He did not see why a congress should not meet and discuss this question, in the interest both of commerce and of Europe. He firmly believed *Principle of freedom must* the principle of this motion would prevail, although *prevail.* it might be resisted by the present administration; for he felt confident that the time would come when the House would not turn a deaf ear to the prayer addressed to it by the great majority of the commercial interests of the country."

Adjourned Debate, March 17.

Mr. Lindsay,* in consequence of the indisposi-
Mr. Lindsay's tion of Mr. Cobden, resumed the ad-
opinion. journed debate —

"In the event of a war, it being clear that all our merchandise would be sent from our shores in the ships of other nations,

---

* Member for Sunderland.

it was equally clear that our shipping would be obliged to lie in our harbors completely unemployed; so that the argument that we required our fleet to protect our commerce and shipping fell to the ground. In the event of a war with France, the merchandise of that country would be conveyed in neutral bottoms, so that our fleet would be of no value in the way supposed. Vast changes had taken place since the last great war. In 1814 the total amount in value of our imports and exports was about 60,000,000*l*. The value in 1860-61 was close upon 300,000,000*l*. Our shipping in 1814 was about 1,000,000 tons; it was now near 5,000,000, of which 500,000 consisted of steamships. Did anybody really suppose that we could have a fleet sufficiently numerous and powerful to protect that vast commerce? If the cry in war was to be 'burn, plunder, and destroy,' we had more to lose than any other nation; and in the event of war, would be by far the largest sufferers."

<small>Our fleet could not protect our commerce.</small>

The lord advocate of Scotland * delivered a clear legal speech, in course of which he asked a question not yet clearly answered, namely: What was to become of blockades, supposing the views of the honorable mover carried —

<small>The lord advocate's opinion.</small>

"The principles advanced by the supporters of the resolution would necessarily lead to the abolition of blockades. The rules of war entitled us to destroy our enemy's commerce. If we gave up that right, could we then maintain the right of blockade, which was an infinitely stronger interference with private property than the right of capture at sea?"

<small>Effect on blockade.</small>

Sir Stafford Northcote † doubted whether the amount of our warehousing-trade and the extent to which our carrying-trade

<small>Sir S. Northcote's opinion.</small>

---

* Mr. Moncrieff, member for Leith. † Member for Stamford.

would be endangered, in the event of war, had been sufficiently considered —

"The phenomena of the last war had been spoken of. But Great Britain would not be able to put down neutrals now. Many close trades which then existed were now thrown open — our colonial trade for example. Commerce always sought the safest ships, and English vessels were then the safest. But the neutral, and not English vessels, would now be the safest. A war with France would threaten our very existence. Both sides would have recourse to neutral vessels. This would cause little injury to France, but the effect on England would be ruinous. Were her majesty's government of opinion that this matter could safely rest where it was? They had rashly concluded certain arrangements with certain powers; while the most important power stood aloof. France would be perfectly safe. All that would be stopped would be British shipping. The government would surely not contend that this treaty might be set aside. Did the noble lord at the head of the government adopt the doctrine that this treaty might be broken as between the nations who might go to war? He apprehended great inconveniences and dangers from the treaty of Paris. In addition to a war with France, that treaty would probably bring us into difficulties with the United States. He thought it impossible to accept the principles laid down by the noble lord at Liverpool, without considering a great many other questions. They all knew that there were stipulations and treaties which war immediately put an end to; but were all treaties made even in contemplation of war to be set aside? If so, they were going back to a state of barbarism. Chancellor Kent said that if a treaty contemplated a state of future war, it preserved its force when the rupture took place; and the obligation of keeping faith, so far from being extinguished, became increased, from the increasing necessity for it. That was a matter which ought to be cleared up; whereas it was now left in studied vagueness.

[Sidenotes: Neutrals could not now be put down. Could matters rest as they were? The Paris declaration binding.]

They had been told that there was no protection for private property on land. The advocates of the Danish claims would be rather startled at such a change of opinion on the part of the government.

Property safe on land— opinion of law officers.

The opinion of her majesty's attorney-general and of the chancellor of the exchequer, last year, was that the claimants who had lost property on land were entitled to have their losses made good; but that there was a broad distinction between property taken on land, and property taken on sea; and that compensation for the latter was not to be given. But what did the Secretary for War* tell them? Why, that this distinction could not for a moment hold water. He had seen it stated that there was a better reason assigned for maritime plunder—that it was more out of sight, and caused less indignation than plunder by land.† There was some truth in that. He did not ignore the humanitarian argument; but, speaking as an Englishman, he thought that the interests of his own country were of all things to be considered. He was not prepared to endorse the views propounded by his honorable friend the mover until

As an Englishman, he would support the motion.

he saw more distinctly how they could be accommodated to the other questions in connection with the subject which they had raised. The advice which was given by Baillie Nicol Jarvie, or rather by his father, to the effect that one should never put his arm out so far that he could not draw it back again, was, he thought, quite applicable under the present circumstances."

Mr. Gower‡ dissented from the motion. *Mr. Gower's dissent.*

Mr. Cave§ expressed his general concurrence with the views of the mover. *Mr. Cave's assent.*

Sir F. Goldsmidt‖ observed that the resolutions of the honorable member for Liverpool would not mitigate the real horrors of war— *Sir F. Goldsmidt's opinion.*

---

* Sir George Lewis.
† See *supra*, p. 11.
‡ Member for Bodmin.
§ Member for Shoreham.
‖ Member for Reading.

"Their only effect would be to relieve our merchants from a somewhat higher rate of marine insurance in time of war. Wars would be best prevented by a firm and temperate policy. Their hardships were unavoidable. But those hardships would be aggravated by our surrender of the right of maritime capture."

Captures not to be relinquished.

Lord Harry Vane* hoped that the motion would not be pressed to a division, though he admitted that the present state of maritime international law was extremely unsatisfactory.

Lord Harry Vane's opinion.
Law now unsatisfactory.

Mr. Buxton † supported the motion. He said that

Mr. Buxton's opinion.

"If the proposition now made were agreed to, we should be able to blockade an enemy's ports with far greater efficiency than at present.‡ We should be able to concentrate our fleets upon the enemy's coasts. At the same time, our enemy, not being equal to us in naval force, could not blockade our ports. His navy would be practically useless to him."

The motion would improve blockades.

Mr. Newdegate § said that when the Paris declaration came to be tested by war, he was afraid that this country would be sorely tempted to set it aside. He trusted that the practical character of the English people would guard them from the delusion of perpetual peace: remembering how many prophecies on this subject had been falsified in the last twelve years.

Mr. Newdegate's opinion.
Paris declaration not binding.

---

* Member for Hastings.   † Member for Maidstone.

‡ What greater interruption to commerce can be imagined than blockades? See the lord advocate's speech, *supra*, p. 67.

§ Member for N. Warwickshire.

Mr. Massey* agreed that the state of international law was unsatisfactory — *Mr. Massey's opinion.*

"Formerly, belligerents carried on war in a form so harsh and oppressive that neutrals suffered almost as much as the enemy, and protested against the tyranny to which they were subjected. This country had sometimes pressed too heavily on neutrals. But it had now gone to the other extreme; and by a sort of self-denying ordinance, had transferred to the neutral the whole advantage. The old system of convoys for merchant ships was exploded. No war hereafter could be greatly protracted. Our ship-owners were treated with derision, as though they were unduly obtruding themselves and their interests. The answer they received was, 'You must submit to the exigencies of war. It is selfish of you to interpose when great interests are at stake.' That was strange language. When we spoke of war, we always had in mind the possibility of a war with France, in which event we should immediately blockade the French ports, and her merchant shipping would immediately disappear from the seas. But then the large war navy of France would prey upon the residue of our commerce not absorbed by neutrals. He could conceive nothing more to the interest of this country than to go to the length which this motion recommended, and thus render the treaty of Paris complete and consistent. It had been denied with great emphasis that in time of war there was any respect for private property on land. That was a new doctrine to him. There was nothing better established than the striking difference between the mode of carrying on war by land and by sea. No country was ever brought to terms of peace by the destruction of its commerce. The military glory of France culminated to its highest point after her flag had disappeared entirely from the seas. It had been said that a treaty might be abrogated by war. But to say that a treaty, specially providing for the exigencies of war, should be annulled in war, would be to repre-

Law now unsatisfactory.

A self-denying ordinance.

The motion would complete the Paris declaration.

War by land and by sea different.

Treaty contemplating war binds in war.

---

* Member for Salford.

sent the powers who were parties to it as acting like children. If one of these powers should attempt to break it, a power so faithless would be visited by the condemnation of Europe; and no advantage would be gained by infraction of the treaty."

<small>Mr. Bentinck's opinion.</small>
<small>Were we bound by the Paris declaration?</small>

Mr. Bentinck* desired to know whether the house or the government meant to say that this country would be bound by the declaration of Paris in the event of war. He would ask his honorable friend not to press his resolution.

<small>Mr. Bright's opinion.</small>

Mr. Bright† remarked, that when the Russian war began, the government advised the Queen to issue the proclamation‡ to which reference had been made more than once—

<small>The old policy untenable.</small>

"That proclamation did precisely what the declaration of Paris two years afterward did for all future wars, should such arise. It was found that the old policy was impossible. Unless you could blockade every port of Russia, American mercantile ships would carry on trade with that country as before the war; and if they had Russian cargoes in those ships, the Americans would not have permitted — he spoke advisedly — without remonstrance,

<small>The Americans would have resisted search.</small>

and probably without resistance, the exercise of a right of search, and the taking from them the property of Russia, then the enemy of England. If the government had not taken the course which they did by the Queen's proclamation of 1854, in six months, or less, we should have been involved in a serious discussion with the United States, which might have ended in adding to the calamity of the then existing war with Russia the calamity of a war with the United States. He held this, after considering the matter, that the course taken by the noble lord§ — for he was

---

* Member from West Norfolk.   ‡ See *infra*, p. 84.
† Member for Birmingham.   § Lord Palmerston.

prime minister in 1856 when the congress met at Paris—was one which he could not have avoided; and as it had become inevitable, it was irrevocable now. The Liverpool chamber of commerce, in a petition which they presented to this house, said that such a proposal as that of the honorable member for Liverpool would shield the shipping interests of this country from greater injury than the fleet of any maritime power could inflict on them in time of war. He agreed that it was wrong to use such language as had been used with respect to the shipping interest, he did not say within the walls of that house, but out of doors. Surely the shipping interest had as great a right to be considered as the great cotton-spinners or the land-owners, or any other great class in the country. The proposal therefore, of the honorable member for Liverpool was one which could not be got rid of by the off-hand declaration of a minister, however influential. The proposal was a very simple one. It merely said, you have freed the cargo, why not include the ships? He anticipated that, instead of provoking war, this proposal would render its occurrence less probable; while if unhappily it did arise, it would be likely to be brought to an earlier termination. At all events, it must be admitted, the proposal was humane and beneficial; and one which followed as a necessary consequence of the Paris declaration. The Secretary for War * had made a speech which he had heard with great surprise and regret. What was it that the jurist Wheaton said on the question as to the fate of treaties in time of war? He said that when treaties were meant to provide for war, it would be against every principle of just interpretation to hold them extinguished by war. So, Dr. Phillimore said that the general maxim that war abrogates treaties must be subject to limitation in one case, namely, the case of treaties which provide for the breaking out of war between the contracting parties. But what was done at Paris in 1856 was not an ordinary treaty, but the general concurrence of the civilized nations of Europe, enacting a new law which should be

Paris declaration unavoidable and irrevocable.

The proposal a sequence to the Paris declaration.

---

* Sir George Lewis.

admitted and accepted in all future time—an agreement which he undertook to say, if the government ever attempted to break, they would call down upon themselves the condemnation of every intelligent man in every intelligent country of the globe."

The solicitor-general* addressed himself, not only to the commercial interests likely to be affected by the proposed change, but also to those moral and patriotic considerations which, though less evident, are deeply involved in the discussion. He said—

The solicitor-general's opinion.

"Two arguments were drawn from the declaration of Paris. In the first place, it was said that there were no reasons in favor of the propositions there laid down which did not equally apply in favor of the proposition of the honorable member for Liverpool. The second argument was, that the effect of the declaration of Paris would be to transfer a large portion of the carrying-trade to neutrals, and to inflict serious injury on our shipping-trade, and on our mercantile interests generally. Those two points embodied the sum and substance of almost all that had been said. The first of those arguments it was not difficult to dispose of. It was easy to show that there were reasons, clear and solid, for that portion of the declaration of Paris as to giving up the right to take enemy's goods out of neutral ships, which would not in any degree whatever apply in favor of the proposition to allow enemy's goods on board enemy's ships or enemy's ships themselves to go free. Neutrals were in a position which, on grounds not only of common justice, but of the mutual interest of belligerents, entitled them to great consideration. The annoyance and disturbance of neutrals by visiting and searching their ships, by interference with their trade, by taking violently away from their ships goods which they had legally and justifiably admitted on board—all these

Two arguments.

The Paris declaration did not support this motion.

---

* Sir Roundell Palmer, who has revised this speech.

were acts in a high degree injurious to persons who
had the strongest claim on the consideration of na- *Neutrals had the strongest claim to consideration.*
tions in amity with them, though at enmity with
each other; and at the same time tended in a high
degree to involve those nations in war with neutrals, and to
draw neutrals, however unwilling, into the contest. Thus there
were various reasons why concessions should be made to neutrals, many of the most important nations of Europe, as well as
the United States of America, having in fact long previously
made treaties bearing on these questions. But it
would be seen that these reasons did not in any *Not to belligerents.*
way operate in favor of making the same concessions
to belligerents. The second argument, as to the transfer of the
carrying-trade to neutrals, was much more important, and involved considerations of much greater difficulty. It must never
be forgotten that governments and nations had to deal with a
balance of evils and inconveniences. The particu-
lar evils which it was supposed would arise from the *The concession to neutrals would do little harm.*
operation of the Paris declaration in favor of neutrals he hoped and believed were greatly exaggerated. But the house would permit him to put before it the
other side of the question, and consider what were the evils
that might arise from the adoption of the principle recommended
by the honorable member for Liverpool. Now, it had been
said that it was of no use to refer to the old established law
of nations, for that we had introduced a new principle by the
declaration of Paris. But that he denied. We had
given up certain belligerent rights, but had intro- *It was not a new principle.*
duced no new principle. But this motion asked us
to give up principles hitherto of cardinal and fundamental importance in the law of nations. If there were any principle of
the law of nations more cardinal than another, it was that in
war governments were identified with their people—that you
could not make war upon the government and have peace with
their people—that the people were bound up with the government and the public interests of the nation, for better or worse.
This principle involved in itself the very highest and most momentous considerations—the interests of patriotism and the inter-

ests of peace. He dreaded to think what might be
the effect of admitting the principle of a political
war and a commercial peace. If anything could
sap the patriotism of a nation, it would be such a state of things.
The merchants of England had on many occasions shown
their patriotism. But under what system had that patriotism
been fostered and maintained? Was it not a system that in
war bound up the English merchants with their government,
which made them fellow-sufferers in its reverses, partners in the
common stake, and looking to its success as the source or return
of their own prosperity? But he ventured to say
that the patriotism of the mercantile class would be
placed in danger if they were indemnified against
the consequences of war, and deprived of their general interest in the maintenance of peace. What was the greatest check we had against unjust and unnecessary wars? Was
it not the burdens they imposed? And if a system were introduced which would admit of carrying on war without those burdens, could it be supposed that the interest of merchants would
be the same as now in preventing war, or in bringing about the
restoration of peace? If the ship-owners should suffer—and he
should regret if they did—by the present state of the law, they
certainly would not have an increased interest in the maintenance of peace if the system of political war and commercial
peace were introduced. But the effect of the change
would be still more important with regard to other
nations whose governments might be more likely to
undertake unjust and aggressive warfare, than with respect to
ourselves. What was the strongest check to wars of aggression
and military ambition? It was the sufferings that must thereby
be entailed, and the fear that the people would not endure them.
But if you made that burden light, you would be giving facilities
to schemes of aggrandizement. The people would become less
vigilant; and by the continuance of trade even the sinews of
war, on which princes depended, would be more easily supplied.
But it was said that what was now asked was to reduce maritime
war to the position into which the progress of civilization had

Danger of the proposed principle.

It would jeopardize the mercantile patriotism.

Suffering is war's best preventive.

brought military warfare. It was perfectly true that
land warfare had received great mitigation; but that
had taken place as much under the influence of considerations of interest as from any mere motives of humanity.
The best way for an army to maintain itself was to be on good
terms with the people of the country which it was occupying.
The commissariat could not get supplies if we were
to apply the principles of marine warfare to operations on land. But no nation had ever done that
with respect to land operations which was now proposed as to
naval warfare. No nation had entered into engagements depriving its generals and armies of the power of taking private
property by land whenever the nature of the operations or the
exigencies of the war might make it necessary or expedient to
do so. There was all the difference in the world between a
moderate use of legal powers and the total renunciation of them.
And the objects of naval operations were different from those of
land warfare. By sea you endeavor to drive off the fleets and
navies—mercantile and warlike—of the enemy. Could any one
say that that had no tendency to cripple him, to bring him to
terms, and to produce a peace? It was evident that
if you adopted this proposal you would deprive
naval warfare of half the field of its operations; and
how could that be done without greatly reducing in
war the strength and importance of a naval as compared with a
military power? What would there be left for our ships to do?
They would be reduced to defensive operations, and,
as has been suggested, to blockades for the purpose
of shutting up the armed vessels of the enemy in
their ports; and, if the enemy's ships did not attempt to come
out a kind of stalemate would be the result. Nor was it possible
to draw a safe line, when maritime power was in question,
between the armed and the mercantile marine of a nation.
Even for the direct purposes of war the mercantile
marine was of the most obvious importance; it was
not only a nursery of seamen, but large merchant
ships might be converted into ships-of-war; merchant ships might be taken up as transports for troops, or for the

Marginal notes: Leniency of land warfare. Ground of this. The proposition would weaken a naval power. Blockade of armed vessels. Mercantile marine formidable in war.

commissariat service; and in case of an invasion they would be more especially available. If we permitted a hostile maritime power to accumulate a great fleet of mercantile vessels, they might be turned against us with the most important results. He would now come to the point of blockade, which was so tenderly touched upon by his honorable friend, the member for Stamford. The honorable member for Liverpool had said he would not interfere with blockade, and other honorable members had said the same. It would, however, be very difficult, upon the principle of this proposition, to save the right of blockading commercial ports. Because what was done by blockading commercial ports? It was obstructing trade; it was destroying the business of great numbers of persons who trade with those ports, and of the inhabitants of those ports, so far as concerns their commerce with foreign nations. Is not that the very thing which was done on the seas when war was made against a mercantile marine? But he foresaw that as soon as the proposition now under discussion was established there would spring up an argument against blockades of this kind. What could be the use of them, it would be said, when your enemy's ships could go to a neutral port, and when, if they put into the Scheldt or Elbe, or some port of Prussia, the railroads would carry the goods over neutral countries much more easily than ships could convey them. It would therefore be said to be a most idle thing to resort to blockades, if they might thus be defeated. The Liverpool petition spoke only of a considerable part of the trade being likely to find its way into neutral hands. That, to some extent, would no doubt be the case. But we could not expect to accomplish the objects of war without suffering serious evils; nor was it clear that it would be for the true interest of peace or civilization if we could. As to the declaration of Paris, we were not likely to go back from it. It could hardly be supposed that the Secretary for War* had meant for a moment that we should think of receding from it. Very lately we had been threatened with

---

* Sir George Lewis.

the danger of war with a power not bound by the declaration of Paris. Was there then, among the merchants of this country, any flinching from that emergency? Did the people of England look that danger in the face as if they were afraid of ruin? No; neither from Liverpool nor Manchester, nor from any other part of the kingdom, did any such timid accents proceed. There was not the least sign, from one end of the kingdom to the other, of any apprehension that the moment we entered into the contest, with the declaration of Paris round our necks, our power would be gone, or our mercantile marine destroyed. {*With it round our necks we felt serene.*} He therefore insisted that we were not wrong in placing faith now as much as heretofore in the patriotism, the resources, and the elasticity of the country."

Mr. Walpole* concurred generally with the views of Sir Roundell Palmer; but expressed strong dissatisfaction with the declaration of Paris. He said— {*Mr. Walpole's opinion.*}

"We have abundant evidence to show that when we entered into the declaration of Paris without the concurrence of America we put our merchants into a position which they ought not to have been compelled to occupy. {*Declaration of Paris mischievous.*} Although we had the finest ships in the Chinese seas, the mere apprehension of a war deprived them of the trade to which they were entitled, and transferred it to the United States because they were not likely to be engaged in hostilities. Could such a state of things be endured without attempting to put the subject on a more satisfactory footing? {*Was it to continue?*} The honorable member for Birmingham told us that the legitimate consequence of the declaration of Paris is that private property shall be pronounced free, even in belligerent ships. His honored and learned friend the solicitor-general had very justly remarked that if we carried the principle so far the same logic will lead to the abolition of commercial blockades. His

---

* The Right Hon. Spencer Horatio Walpole, member for Cambridge University.

He desired an answer.

object in rising was to elicit from the government whether this one-sided declaration was to be amended and placed on a better footing."

Lord Palmerston's opinion.

Lord Palmerston had no hesitation in saying that to go back to the parties who assembled at Paris, and to ask them to rescind those resolutions would be a course which no gentleman could seriously think the government was likely to adopt, or that, if adopted, the government was likely to get the other parties to agree to it—

Repeal of the Paris declaration impossible.

The motion, no logical deduction from it.

"The proposition made by the honorable member for Liverpool, that we should agree that private property by sea should be exempt from capture, was said to be a logical deduction from the declaration of Paris. He denied that proposition. The declaration of Paris related entirely to the relations between belligerents and neutrals. The proposition of the honorable member related to the relations of belligerents to each other. The honorable member for Birmingham had been kind enough to attach some value to opinions which he (Lord Palmerston) had expressed some years ago at Liverpool.* The attention which he had been pleased to pay, and the weight which he had been pleased to give to his (Lord Palmerston's) opinion, induced him to hope that he would with him (Lord Palmerston) alter the opinion which had been then expressed. His opinion, therefore, distinctly was, that if you give up that power which you possess, and which all maritime states possess and have exercised—of taking the ships, the property, and the crews of the nation with whom you may happen to be at war, you would be crippling the right arm of our strength. You would be inflicting a blow upon our naval power, and you would be guilty of an act of political suicide. He hoped the honorable gentleman would be content with the discussion he had raised on the question, and withdraw his resolution."

His lordship's Liverpool opinions.

The motion suicidal.

---

* See *supra*, p. 56.

Mr. Disraeli said that by the declaration of Paris we had given up the cardinal principle of our maritime power— *Mr. Disraeli's opinion.*

"There is a general impression that the great change made in the maritime code may be, perhaps must be, the cause of serious results to the maritime power of this country. He thought it not at all a question of the shipping interest only; it concerns the whole maritime strength of this country, if it is true that we have acknowledged the principle that the flag of a neutral covers the cargo. This must divert the commerce of the country in time of war into neutral bottoms; and that, he believed, will have dealt a serious blow to our maritime strength. It was said that on the eve of war with Russia we feared that the assertion of our old principle might involve us in embarrassments with the United States. The noble lord recognized the accuracy of that description. How could we maintain our system of blockades, if we conceded the principle which the honorable mover recommended? If we could not maintain our blockades, it was evident that our naval power must cease to be aggressive, and exist only for purposes of defence." *The new rule as to the neutral flag a death-blow to us.* *The motion would make blockades unavailing.*

Mr. Horsfall, in deference to the suggestions made from both sides of the House, withdrew the motion; his object having been abundantly attained by the delivery of the preceding opinions, which came seasonably, at the very moment when the "chief points" had been brought to a close. *Motion withdrawn.*

APPENDIX.

THE PARIS "SOLEMN DECLARATION,"
April 16, 1856.

The Paris declaration. The plenipotentiaries who signed the Treaty of Paris of the 30th of March, 1856, assembled in conference—considering:

That maritime law, in time of war, has long been the subject of deplorable disputes;

That the uncertainty of the law and of the duties in such a matter, gives rise to differences of opinion between neutrals and belligerents, which may occasion serious difficulties, and even conflicts;

That it is consequently advantageous to establish a uniform doctrine on so important a point;

That the plenipotentiaries assembled in congress at Paris, cannot better respond to the intentions by which their governments are animated, than by seeking to introduce into international relations fixed principles in this respect—

The above-named plenipotentiaries, being duly authorized, resolved to concert among themselves as to the means of attaining this object; and having come to an agreement, have adopted the following solemn declaration:

1. Privateering is, and remains abolished;
2. The neutral flag covers enemy's goods, with the exception of contraband of war;

3. Neutral goods, with the exception of contraband of war, are not liable to capture under enemy's flag;

4. Blockades, in order to be binding, must be effective; that is to say, maintained by a force sufficient really to prevent access to the coast of the enemy.

The governments of the undersigned plenipotentiaries engage to bring the present declaration to the knowledge of the states which have not taken part in the Congress of Paris, and to invite them to accede to it.

Convinced that the maxims which they now proclaim cannot but be received with gratitude by the whole world, the undersigned plenipotentiaries doubt not that the efforts of their governments to obtain the general adoption thereof will be crowned with full success.

The present declaration is not, and shall not be binding, except between those powers who have acceded, or shall accede to it.

Done at Paris, the 16th of April, 1856.

(Signed)

Buol-Schauenstein.	Hatzfeldt.
Hübner.	Orloff.
Walewski.	Brunnow.
Bourqueney.	Cavour.
Clarendon.	De Villamarina.
Cowley.	Aali.
Manteuffel.	Mehemmed Djemil.

THE QUEEN'S PROCLAMATION,
MAY 13, 1861.

VICTORIA R.,

Whereas hostilities have unhappily commenced between the government of the United States of America and certain states styling themselves the Confederate States of America;

The Queen's proclamation.

And whereas we, being at peace with the government of the United States, have declared our royal determination to maintain a strict and impartial neutrality in the contest between the said contending parties;

We, therefore, have thought fit, by and with the advice of our Privy Council, to issue this our royal proclamation;

And we do hereby strictly charge and command all our loving subjects to observe a strict neutrality in and during the aforesaid hostilities, and to abstain from violating or contravening either the laws and statutes of the realm in this behalf, or the law of nations in relation thereto, as they will answer to the contrary at their peril.

And whereas in and by a certain statute* made and passed in the 59th year of his majesty King George III, entitled "An act to prevent the enlisting or engagement of his majesty's subjects to serve in a foreign service, and the fitting out or

---

* 59th Geo. 3, c. 69.

equipping in his majesty's dominions vessels for warlike purposes, without his majesty's license," it is, among other things, declared and enacted as follows:*

Now, in order that none of our subjects may unwarily render themselves liable to the penalties imposed by the said statute, we do hereby strictly command that no person or persons whatsoever do commit any act, matter, or thing whatsoever, contrary to the provisions of the said statute, upon pain of the several penalties by the said statute imposed, and of our high displeasure.

And we do hereby further warn all our loving subjects, and all persons whatsoever entitled to our protection, that if any of them shall presume, in contempt of this our royal proclamation, and of our high displeasure, to do any acts in derogation of their duty as subjects of a neutral sovereign, in the said contest, or in violation or contravention of the law of nations in that behalf; as for example, and more especially, by entering into the military service of either of the said contending parties as commissioned or non-commissioned officers or soldiers; or by serving as officers, sailors, or marines, on board any ship or vessel of war or transport, of or in the service of either of the said contending parties; or by engaging to go or going to any place beyond the seas with intent to enlist or engage in any such service, or by procuring or

---

* For the verbose enactments of this act, see the Statute Book. Sir Roundell Palmer, in his speech, *infra*, p. 88, says "they are sufficiently set out in the title."

attempting to procure, within her majesty's dominions at home or abroad, others to do so; or by fitting out, arming or equipping any ship or vessel to be employed as a ship-of-war or privateer or transport, by either of the said contending parties; or by breaking or endeavoring to break any blockade lawfully and actually established by or on behalf of either of the said contending parties; or by carrying officers, soldiers, dispatches, arms, military stores, or materials, or any article or articles considered and deemed to be contraband of war according to the law or modern usage of nations, for the use or service of either of the said contending parties, all persons so offending will incur and be liable to the several penalties and penal consequences by the said statute, or by the law of nations, in that behalf imposed or denounced.

And we do hereby declare that all our loving subjects, and persons entitled to our protection, who may misconduct themselves in the premises, will do so at their peril and of their own wrong, and that they will in nowise obtain any protection from us against any liabilities or penal consequences, but will, on the contrary, incur our high displeasure by such misconduct.

Given, etc., 13th May, 1861.

GOD SAVE THE QUEEN.

SIR ROUNDELL PALMER'S SPEECH ON THE EFFECT OF THE QUEEN'S PROCLAMATION.*

The O'Donoghue moved for returns of the number of vessels that had during the past six months broken the blockade of the southern ports of America. He complained that the British government had not taken steps to prevent breaches of that blockade, which was not in his opinion, to be held ineffective merely because the Americans "had not been able to accomplish an impossibility, viz: the hermetically sealing of 3,000 miles of coast." The honorable mover further insisted that the government ought to enforce the Queen's proclamation against furnishing the belligerents with articles contraband of war.

Sir Roundell Palmer (solicitor-general): I think it desirable that a few words should be said to correct a total misapprehension of a matter of law, into which the honorable gentleman opposite has fallen. He implies, by the terms of his notice of motion, and more distinctly stated in his speech, that all masters of British merchant vessels who may have run the blockade with articles contraband of war on board have been guilty of illegal acts, in violation of her majesty's proclamation, which the government of this country, having their attention called to them, ought to have in-

---
* Revised. *Times*, 21st February, 1862.

terfered to prevent, but had not done so. He has
also suggested that the authorities of the port of
Nassau must be subject to serious blame for having permitted ships under similar circumstances
to call at that port and to take in supplies, and to
have the benefit of calling and remaining there
when they had on board articles contraband of
war, which the honorable gentlemen seemed to
suppose that her majesty's proclamation had made
it illegal for them to have on board, and which
therefore they could not be permitted to carry
without a violation of neutrality. In all these
respects the honorable gentleman has totally misunderstood the law. This country is governed by
law, and except as far as her majesty's government have powers by law to control the action of
private British subjects, whether masters of ships
or others, of course they are perfectly powerless
in the matter. The only law which enables her
majesty's government to interfere in such cases is
that commonly called the foreign enlistment act,
and the whole nature and scope of that act is sufficiently and shortly set out in the title. It is "an
act to prevent the enlistment and engagement of
her majesty's subjects to serve in foreign service,
and the fitting out or equipping in her majesty's
dominions vessels for warlike purposes without
her majesty's license." That act does not touch
in any way whatever private merchant vessels,
which may carry cargoes, contraband or not contraband, between this country or any of the dominions of her majesty and any port in a bel-

ligerent country, whether under blockade or not; and the government of this country, and the governments of our colonial possessions, have no power whatever to interfere with private vessels under such circumstances. It is perfectly true that in the Queen's proclamation there is a general warning, addressed to all the Queen's subjects, that they are not, either in violation of their duty to the Queen as subjects of a neutral sovereign, or in violation and contravention of the law of nations, to do various things, one of which is carrying articles considered and deemed to be contraband of war according to law or the modern usages of nations, for the use or service of either of the contending parties. That warning is addressed to them to apprise them that if they do these things they will have to undergo the penal consequences by the statute or by the law of nations in that behalf imposed or denounced. In those cases in which the statute is silent,* the government are powerless, and the law of nations comes in. The law of nations exposes such persons to have their ships seized and their goods taken and subjected to confiscation, and it further deprives them of the right to look to the government of their own country for any protection. And this principle of non-interference in things which the law does not enable the government to deal with, so far from being a violation of the duty of neutrality—which the government are

---

* The statute is silent as to contraband and blockade.

sincerely anxious to comply with — is in accordance with all the principles which have been laid down by jurists, and more especially by the great jurists of the United States of America. In order that the honorable gentleman may understand exactly how the case stands, I may be permitted to read a short passage from one of the works of these writers. Wheaton, who, as everybody knows, has written one of the most valuable treatises on the subject that ever was composed says —

"It is not the practice of nations to undertake to prohibit their own subjects, by previous laws, from trafficking in articles contraband of war. Such trade is carried on at the risk of those engaged in it, under the liabilities and penalties prescribed by the law of nations, or particular treaties."

Wheaton then goes on to justify the conduct of the United States in not interfering to prevent the supply of arms to Texas, then at war with Mexico, and says—

"The government is not bound to prevent it, and could not have prevented it without a manifest departure from the principle of neutrality, and is in no way answerable for the consequences."

Chancellor Kent, in his scarcely less admirable work, says —

"It is a general understanding that the powers at war may seize and confiscate all contraband goods, without any complaint on the part of the neutral merchant, and without any imputation of a breach of neutrality in the neutral sovereign himself. It was contended, on the part of the French nation in 1796, that neutral governments were bound to restrain their subjects from selling or exporting articles contraband of war to the belligerent powers. But it was successfully shown, on the part of the United States, that neutrals may lawfully sell at home to a belligerent purchaser, or carry themselves to the belligerent powers contraband articles, subject to the right of seizure *in transitu*. This right has since been explicitly declared by the judicial authorities of this country. The right of the neutral to transport, and of the hostile power to seize, are conflicting rights, and neither party can charge the other with a criminal act."

I think, therefore, it is very clear that the government at home, and the colonial authorities at Nassau, have taken the only course which it was possible to take consistently with the law of the land, which they were bound in any case to follow, or with the recognized principles and customs of international law, and more especially with those principles and customs as recognized and acted upon by the United States themselves.

THE QUEEN'S WAIVER OF RIGHT ON THE EVE OF THE RUSSIAN WAR, 28TH MARCH, 1854.

Her majesty, the Queen of the united kingdom of Great Britain and Ireland, having been compelled to take up arms in support of an ally, is desirous of rendering the war as little onerous as possible to the powers with whom she remains at peace.

The Queen's waiver as to neutral flag.

To preserve the commerce of neutrals from all unneccessary obstruction, her majesty is willing, for the present, to waive a part of the belligerent rights appertaining to her by the law of nations.

It is impossible for her majesty to forego her right of seizing articles contraband of war, and of preventing neutrals from bearing the enemy's dispatches; and she must maintain the right of a belligerent to prevent neutrals from breaking any effective blockade which may be established with an adequate force against the enemy's forts, harbors, or coasts.

But her majesty will waive the right of seizing enemy's property laden on board a neutral vessel, unless it be contraband of war.

It is not her majesty's intention to claim the confiscation of neutral property, not being contraband of war, found on board enemy's ships; and her majesty further declares, that being anxious to lessen as much as possible the evils of war and to restrict its operations to the regularly organized forces of the country, it is not her present intention to issue letters of marque for the commissioning of privateers.

SIR WILLIAM MOLESWORTH'S SPEECH ON THE NEUTRAL FLAG.*

On the 4th July, 1854, Sir William Molesworth delivered, in the House of Commons, a most learned and powerful speech in support of the maxim, "free ships make free goods." He showed that the opposite rule of the Consolato del Mare was early and largely dissented from. "At various times," said Sir William,† "the great majority of European states have been induced to condemn the rule of capturing enemy's goods on board neutral ships, and to expunge that rule from the public law of Europe. The first English treaty which contains the principle 'free ships, free goods' was that of Westminster, in 1654, between the King of Portugal and Oliver Cromwell. It continued in force till 1810, that is for 156 years. In 1655, the lord protector concluded a similar treaty with Louis XIV. How long it continued in force I am unable to say, but in 1677 the rule 'free ships, free goods' was inserted in the treaty of St. Germain en Laye, and was the rule of our amicable relations with France for the next 116 years. From 1677 till 1793 the all but invariable rule of our friendly intercourse with France was that free ships should give freedom to goods. The first of our treaties with

Sir William Molesworth on neutral flag.

---

* Abridged from *Hansard*.
† Replying to Mr. John George Phillimore.

Spain which contained this principle was that of 1665. From that period till 1796, thirteen treaties were concluded with Spain, in every one of which there is an article which either expressly declares that free ships shall give freedom to goods, or renews a treaty which contains that position. In our treaties with the United Provinces the invariable rule of our intercourse from 1667 to 1780 was, that the ships of the United Provinces should make free the goods of the enemies of England. The treaties between England and the great maritime powers of Western Europe show that between 1654 and 1793 the all but invariable rule was 'free ships, free goods.' I must, however, admit that the theory of the great maritime powers as expressed in treaties was at variance with their practice during war. The reason is obvious. During peace men's minds have a tendency to conform to what ought to be the rule of international law. But in war passion, hatred, and seeming necessity and the fancied interest of the moment are apt to determine the actions of powerful belligerents who, often relying on their might, set at defiance the best established rules of war. Every one of the great maritime powers has repeatedly treated neutrals as subjects; and has confiscated not only enemy's goods on board neutral ships, but neutral ships for containing enemy's goods, and has even prohibited all neutral commerce with enemies. Nor has this country shown greater respect than our neighbors for the rights of neutrals. By means of fictitious blockades we have repeatedly claimed the right of stopping the trade of neutrals with our enemies. I must acknowledge the rule free ships, free goods, is not contained in some of the treaties between the northern and western powers. But I have shown that the general rule of amicable intercourse, as established by treaty between the northern and western powers, with the exception of England — between the United States and the old and the new world, and between the Ottoman Porte and the great powers of Europe was free ships, free goods. I am, therefore, entitled to assert that though it has been the usage to act upon the rule of capturing enemy's goods on board neutral ships, yet that usage has been, and still is held by the great majority of civilized nations to be at variance with correct notions of what is right and just. It is said that the fact that so many treaties contain the rule free ships, free goods, and so few the rule of confiscating enemy's goods on board neutral ships proves that the latter rule was the general rule of public law. The friends of the extension of neutral rights do not deny that this was the general rule of the public law of England, and of many other nations. They merely assert that it ought not to be the rule of international law, and that it is contrary to the opinions of the majority of civilized nations."

INDEX.

	PAGE
Ad libitum doctrine of contraband	25
Afghanistan, destruction of fruit trees in	4
Alexander, the Czar, defensive destruction of property by	7
American Colonies, rebellion of	15
American war, regularity of	15
Arbitration—See Mediation.	
Arms, etc., whether war is prolonged by	20
Asylum given by neutrals to belligerents	17
Atherton, Sir W., as to immunity to private property	62
Attorney-General—see Atherton, Sir W.	
Bajazet, a prisoner of war	6
Baring, Mr. T., M. P., immunity to private property at sea	66
Belligerents in their enemy's country—(see Table of Contents, sec. i)	1
in their own country—(see Table of Contents, sec. ii)	7
at sea—(see Table of Contents, sec. iii)	9
Belligerents and Neutrals—(see Table of Contents, sec. iv)	14
Bentinck, Mr., M. P., as to immunity to private property	72
Blockades—(see Table of Contents, sec. vi)	27
Paris declarations as to	51
Queen's proclamation as to	51
Bowyer, Sir G., M. P., as to immunity to private property	63
Brienne, General, at the siege of Almeida	4
Bright, Mr., M. P., as to immunity to private property	72
Brougham, Lord, as to shortening wars by early severities	2
the burning of Joan of Arc (note)	6
the origin of law of nations (note)	29
Brune, Marshal, as to destruction of the Dutch dikes	3
Burke, Mr., as to the treatment of a conquered province, etc	3
as to defence of towns	9
Buxton, Mr., M. P., immunity to private property	70
Bynkershoek, as to the treatment of prisoners	6

INDEX.

	PAGE
Captors, encouragement to	41–43
Cave, Mr., as to immunity to private property	69
Changes in the maritime law of nations — (see Table of Contents, sec. viii and ix)	44
Charleston stone fleet	5
Children, consideration for, during war	5
Civil law not the foundation of the law of nations	28
Cochrane, Mr. B., as to immunity to private property	63
Committee of Commons as to immunity of private property	58
Commons, House of, present state of sentiment in, as to immunity to private property at sea during war — (see Table of Contents, sec. x)	61
Opinion of Committee of	58
Contraband of war—See Table of Contents, sec. v.	
Its principle examined	19–22
Costs and damages when given to neutrals	41
when awarded against captors, usually paid by government	42
Crimea, the war in	4–5
Danger, the test of efficiency of blockade	32
Declaration of Paris, 1856, does not define contraband	25
silent as to stoppage and search	25
See Table of Contents, sec. viii.	
Defence of towns	8
Derby, Lord, as to binding force of the Declaration of Paris	45
Diebitsch, Count, his conduct in Roumelia in 1829	2
Disraeli, Mr., as to immunity to private property	81
Edinburgh Review quoted, as to Lord Stowell	37, 38
Ellenborough, Lord, as to contraband	23
Fire-arms, etc., do they prolong war?	20
Fishing-boats of enemy	12
Fortified town, defence of	8
Forts, etc., whether they may be destroyed during war	4
"Free ships, free goods," established by the Declaration of Paris	47
Sir W. Molesworth's speech as to	93
Goldsmidt, Sir F., as to immunity to private property	69
Gower, Mr., as to immunity to private property	69
Granville, Earl, as to contraband	23
Declaration of Paris	46
the adoption of the maxim "Free ships, free goods"	51
Gulliver, advice of, to the King of Brobdignag (note)	22

INDEX.

	PAGE
Harbors may not always be closed by owners	8
Hautefeuille, M., as to deeming wars just (note)	16
the freedom of enemy's goods under neutral flag	48
Hawkwood, Sir John	8
Hobbes (note)	39
Horner, Mr., his opinion of Lord Stowell	39
Horsfall, Mr., M. P., his motion as to private property at sea	61
Hume, David, as to gunpowder	21
Italian war of 1859, respect to private property	3
Intermission of blockade	33
Jacopo del Verme, destruction of the dikes of the Adige by	8
Joan of Arc (note)	6
Just war, what must be so deemed	16
Kent, Chancellor, as to difference between land and sea warfare	11
Kingsdown, Lord, as to contraband	23
encouragement to captors	43
costs and damages to neutrals	44
Law of nations characterized	1
Lawrence, Mr., as to Lord Stowell	40
Leniency and forbearance on land now enjoined on belligerents — not so at sea	2
Lewis, Sir G. C., as to immunity to private property	65
Licenses to trade with enemy (note)	55
Liddell, Mr., as to immunity to private property	63
Lindsey, Mr., as to do.	66
Lord Advocate—(see Moncrieff, Mr.)	
Louis XIV, his destruction of the Dutch dikes	4
his treatment of prisoners	5
Low Countries, revolt of, against Spain	4
Lushington, Dr., as to costs and damages to neutrals	42
as to destruction of enemy's merchant vessels	10
Maritime law of nations, license given by it for plunder (see the Table of Contents, sec. iii)	9
Maritime law of nations, its partiality to belligerents	19
late changes in —(see Table of Contents, sec. viii)	44
proposed changes in —(see Table of Contents, sec. ix)	61
Massey, Mr., a passage in his history considered	15
as to right of searching ships under convoy (note)	40
as to immunity to private property during war	71

	PAGE
Mediation, protocol as to (note)	53
Medicinal plants deemed contraband	24
Merchants' opinions as to immunity to private property	58
Molesworth, Sir W., speech on the neutral flag	93
Moncrieff, Mr., as to immunity to private property	67
Napoleon I, as to immunity to private property	55
Napoleon III	6
Nations, law of. See Law of Nations, Maritime Law of Nations, etc.	
Neutrals, position of, during war—(see Table of Contents, sec. iv)	16
must hold regular war just	16
asylum granted by, to belligerent vessels	17
must not assist belligerents	19
may trade with them	19
restriction	20
ships of, liable to stoppage and search—(see Table of Contents, sec. v)	22
costs and damage to	41
Neutrals and belligerents—(see Table of Contents, sec. iv)	14
Neutral goods under enemy's flag exempted from capture by the Paris declaration	51
Newdegate, Mr., as to immunity to private property	70
Northcote, Sir S., as to immunity to private property	67
Odessa, bombardment of	4
supposed case as to	8
Orders in Council bind the Prize Court	37–40
of 1807	38
Palmer, Sir Roundell, as to blockades	32
speech as to immunity to private property at sea	74
speech as to the Queen's proclamation	87
Palmerston, Lord, as to the maxim "Free ships, free goods"	49
Palmerston, Lord, as to proposed immunity to enemy's merchant ships	54, 56, 80
Paper Blockades	30
Paris Declarations. See Declaration of Paris and Table of Contents, sec. viii.	
Peter the Great, defensive destruction of property by	7
Phillimore, Dr., as to the Orders in Council of 1807	38
Prisoners of war	6
Privateering abolished by the Paris declaration	46
not by the United States	46

CONTENTS.

	PAGE
Prize, becomes the captors'....................................	43
as a mode of remuneration...............................	34
Prize court bound to obey one of the litigants before it.........37,	40
Prize jurisdiction—(see Table of Contents, sec. vii)..............	35
Proclamation of the Queen as to contraband.....................	22
as to blockades.................. 27,	31
set out....	87
Property of enemy on land how treated........................	2
at sea, how treated—(see Table of Contents, sec. iii)....	10
Proposal that it should not be liable to capture—(see Table of Contents, sec. ix).......	52
Protocol as to Mediation (note).................................	53
Provisions, when contraband..............................22,	23
Quasi-contraband..	24
Regular war must be deemed just; *quære*	16
Revival of blockade...	33
Roman law not the foundation of the law of nations (note)........	28
Russell, Earl, as to Paris declaration............................	45
as to immunity to enemy's private property	59
Sarrazin, General, as to destruction of Fort of Almeida.......... .	5
Scott, Sir William. See Stowell, Lord.	
Search..	25
Solferino, the battle of...	6
Solicitor-General. See Palmer, Sir Roundell.	
Spain, revolt of Low Countries against..........................	14
Stoppage to search for contraband..............................	25
to ascertain national character.......................	26
Stowell, Lord, his position and conduct characterized............	38
his judgments as to prize jurisdiction contrasted..35–38	
revision of judgments by (note)...................	24
his rules as to costs and damages to neutrals.......	41
corrected by Privy Council.......................	43
as to when enemy's property may be destroyed.....	10
as to enemy's fishing-boats.......................	12
as to contraband.................................	24
as to blockade....................................	30
Story, Mr. Justice, as to blockade...............................	31
Timour...	6
Towns, mercantile, defence of...................................	9
fortified, defence of.....................................;	9
Trade between neutrals and belligerents.........................	19

	PAGE
Vane, Lord H., as to immunity to private property	70
Vattel, as to leniency in war	2
as to conduct of belligerents in their own country	7
as to deeming wars just (note)	16
Visitation. See S oppage.	
Voltaire, as to destruction of the Dutch dikes by Louis XIV	4
Waiver, by the Queen, of right, on eve of the Russian war, set out	92
Walpole, Mr., as to immunity to private property	79
War, modern practice of, different from ancient	1
what property respected during	4
must be regular to give belligerent rights	14
if regular, whether to be deemed just	16
Wellington, Duke of, his respect for private property in war	2
Wheaton, Mr., his remarks as to Lord Stowell	40
William the Silent, defensive destruction of property by	7
Women, consideration for, during war	5
York, Duke of, proposed destruction of the Dutch dikes by	3

www.ingramcontent.com/pod-product-compliance
Lightning Source LLC
Chambersburg PA
CBHW020141170426
43199CB00010B/834